I'm Not A Celebrity but I Have A Story

Chenelle M. Wiles

This publication may not be reproduced, stored in a retrieval system, transmitted into any other forms such as mechanical, electronic, recording, photocopying, or otherwise, without written permission of the publisher.

Copyright © 2011 by Chenelle M. Wiles

All rights reserved, Published by Chenelle M. Wiles

Printed in the United States of America

Second Edition

ISBN 978-0-578-13856-5

I dedicate this book to the memory of my maternal grandmother Shirley Y. Washington; your memory lives on through your family and friends, I love and thank you for paving the way for me and so many others!!!

To my son and young man Demontay; I am so proud of you, continue to succeed, and know that I love you very much!!!!!

For my God sister LaShawn T. Summers; this is a tribute to you, thank you for always being there for me and loving me unconditionally, I love you!!!

Washington D.C., Maryland, & North Carolina; stay on the grind and never stop pushing, I'm doing it for all of us!!!

Contents

Acknowledgements   *1*

1. Growing Up   *5*
2. Giving Back   *28*
3. Relationships   *46*
4. New Life (D.A.W.)   *72*
5. Recovery   *102*

****LIFE****   *125*

Acknowledgements

Saturday morning of July 5, 1980 at George Washington University in Washington D.C., I entered this world not knowing what was in store for the life ahead of me. I acknowledge first and foremost my Lord and Savior, for He continues to bless me and nothing is possible without Him! A lot of molding had to take place and I had my work cut out for me. Struggles came in my path so many times and to this day of course I still encounter struggles, but my struggles will never define me. I've accomplished a lot of successful admirations and writing this book is a wonderful accomplishment that I've been blessed to do! There are so many people I credit my success to and I wouldn't be here without my Lord and Savior; I give Him all the thanks and credit! My parents Katrine H. Wiles and Theodore J. Wiles; for taking the time out to create and mold me; I'm thankful for you and I love you! My five siblings Anthone, Sheriliah, Nise, Netra, and Sir Gordon: I'm proud of all of you for being successful and always doing what it takes for yourselves to stay strong, I truly thank God for all of you and I love all of you dearly! For my maternal grandparents: my maternal grandmother Shirley Y. Washington (R.I.P); I miss you so much and have wonderful memories of how you worked so hard to keep our family together, I will forever keep you in my heart and your memory lives on through me and many other family members! My maternal grandfather William Howard; God put you in our family for a special reason, I'm very thankful for everything you bring to everyone you surround! You're truly a blessing and I'm blessed to be your oldest granddaughter! I'm thankful for my maternal great grandmother Martha Howard; my grandfather got his strong will from you, may you R.I.P. My Godmother Leslie; I thank you for always being there for me and encouraging me to keep my faith in the Lord, I love you! Two other people who've been Godparents to me as well as inspirations in my life are Mr. and Mrs. David and Carolyn Turner; you two have been so supportive and loving, I thank you so much for being who you are! To all of my lovely nephews and nieces: Elijiah, Samara, Anthony, Amena, Amerie, Abby, Mya, Destiny, and Millie. Auntie loves all of you and my desire for all of you is to succeed and never let yourselves down! I'm thankful for all of my precious God children! My lovely son Demontay; for you I have worked so hard for and want the very best for you. No matter what you've been through, always acknowledge the fact that you're a blessing and God has a plan for you (it's up to you to put that plan into action)! I love you so much and want you to never stop succeeding in life! My God sister Natasha; you're encouraging words and unconditional love is what I love so much about you! As I've gotten older we've grown closer and our bond is sent from God, I love you so much and appreciate you! I have to dedicate so much of my success to my awesome God sister Shawn; you've been there for me since day one. Your teaching skills were implemented to me at a very young age and you've always given everything your all regardless of how tough things were. I can't thank you enough for your unconditional love and support, God knew what He was doing when he put you in my life, I love you! Special thanks to Trisha and the Norket family, Reynolds/Isley's, Wilson's, Vincent's/Costin's, Gibson's, Stokes/Williams/Gaines, Little's/Summers, Miller's, Tinsley's and to all of my friends especially Robyn, Nikki, Michelle, Kim, Regina, Laquista, April, Dwana, Alicia, Clianda, and Olympia! If I didn't acknowledge someone, I apologize and appreciate you as well. I appreciate all of my family members for your support; the Washington's, Howard's, Johnson's, and Wiles' Families! My younger people I've mentored and continue to mentor(i.e. Tiaera and Patrice); I thank all of you for helping me bring out the youth in me! Special thanks to my home church family (Charlotte North Carolina) formerly known as Jackson Park Baptist Church and expanded into what is now, Steele Creek Church of Charlotte. Special thanks to my pastor Kelvin Smith; who has been at the church since I began attending which was in my pre-teen years; you've been a wonderful man of God and I thank you for everything! There are so many other wonderful people from Steele Creek who I am so thankful for: David Wallace, Amy Smith (pastor's wife), Bob Poole, Regina and Andre Cureton, Ashaki and Willie McNeil, Sean and Sharon Murphy, Park and Tammy Gillespie, and so many others. Thanks to any and all teachers and professors that helped me in school (i.e. Selwyn Elementary, Alexander Graham Middle School, Myers Park High School, West Charlotte High School, and North Carolina Agricultural and Technical State University). I send out a large thank you to all of the teachers, school faculty, therapists, and Social Workers who have helped and continue to help my son (i.e. Eastern Guilford Middle School, Eastern Guilford High School, Northeast Guilford High School, and Sue Kirkman). Thanks to my past and present coworkers; stay motivated for the right reasons. I am also thankful for my Greensboro North Carolina church family, Wells Memorial C.O.G.I.C.

    Anything is possible especially when strong will and

dedication are put together. At the time I started on this book I was diagnosed with Carpal Tunnel Syndrome, and according to the National Institutes of Health it is pain, tingling, and other problems in the hand caused by pressure on the median nerve. Two weeks prior I was involved in an automobile accident. It was early on a Tuesday morning around 6:40 a.m. and I was on my way to work, I had to be at work by 7:00 a.m. Another motorist ran a red light while I was proceeding through my traffic light, and that's how the collision happened. I got banged up on the right side of my body; damage was mostly done to my right wrist and hand. I had to wear a brace on my wrist for a few weeks, but that certainly wouldn't stop me. The important thing is that I have my life and for that I'm truly thankful. Just taking my free time to write this book was a gift in itself, because I knew I'd be able to share a lot of myself with others through this book. Although I was very uncomfortable at times while writing, I felt a sense of pride because I knew I was putting together a fabulous masterpiece! Having to wear a brace on my arm didn't stop me from doing my regular daily activities which involved attending sporting events for my son and other young children I mentored, or even playing with my toddler twin nieces (Amena and Amerie) whom resided with me at the time(as well as my sister Nise). All this meant was that I had to be a little more careful and utilize patience!

1. Growing Up

What are the odds of beating the odds in life? I've probably asked myself this question a million times in my life. Growing up and overcoming many obstacles is just a part of the human nature, well at least that's what I learned when I became an adult. When I was a child, I thought I was the only person in the world who couldn't get anywhere in life. My mother has always been an intelligent woman especially in math; I used to always think she was a genius when it came to numbers. Everyone is blessed with different talents and skills in life; we should all do ourselves the best thing possible by going after our callings. For me growing up in a big family with four younger siblings, I endured major responsibilities. I started out taking on motherly duties around the age of ten. Although I went through losing a lot of time hanging out with friends, doing afterschool activities, and even enjoying free time, I loved being around my siblings. I can recall teaching one of my siblings (Nise) how to ride a bike. I felt lucky to be the person who taught her that skill, and it was more rewarding seeing her happy and excited to be able to ride a bike without training wheels at the age of four. Now today I look at that particular sister and how she mothers her young twin daughters, certain things I used to do with her she does the same with them today. Many and most siblings have physical altercations but I can honestly say I've never gotten into a physical altercation with any of my siblings besides minor hits here and there. We've had our days of disagreements but somehow we never came to blows. I do recall one of my sisters whom follows closest to me in age;

Chenelle M. Wiles

Sheriliah and I both would sometimes team up against our older brother when we had arguments, but he would be solo. We were at home during summer vacation from school and our mother was at work. I'm not sure what the argument was about but my brother made us mad so we got into it with him. Licks and hits were exchanged but it wasn't like a full blown out fight. My mother was either called or she called us checking on us like she did on a daily basis. Either way it went, she came home and all three of us got beat down by her. I laugh at it right now because I can remember the scene so well. We were living in Charlotte North Carolina in a four bedroom housing authority owned apartment. The apartment was two levels but wasn't very big at all. Our beat down was handed to us in our laundry room area right beside the downstairs bathroom, right in front of the washer and dryer. I think most children feel as though parents are the cruelest people on earth when physical punishment comes into play. I certainly felt that way a lot, but that's just the mindset of a child. I didn't get into much trouble for getting into conflicts or even getting into trouble in school. The times I was spanked or hit was when I expressed myself about not wanting to babysit my siblings, oh and those times I thought I was going to need to be hospitalized. My mother raised six children on her own and I'm sure it was tough; she often had assistance in the home from me and some of my other siblings (after I left for college). She raised two men and with that said, she had to be a mother and a father at times. My

Growing Up

parents were married and lived together for a little while when I was younger; so I did have both of them along with my older brother and younger sister, during my earlier years of life. Living in Landover Maryland surrounded by a lot of family mostly the maternal side, was wonderful. My maternal grandmother and maternal grandfather have always been there for our family. Even though my grandparents were divorced, I saw and spent a lot of time with both of them. My grandmother took care of my cousins, myself, and two siblings a lot of the time and took us on a lot of trips. She kept us while our parents were either working or weren't around at the time. One of my older cousins on my maternal side, I saw him a lot when I was younger due to the fact we were usually at my grandmother's house. His father and my grandmother were siblings, his mother passed away when he was very young in a car accident, so my grandmother raised him. I looked up to him a lot because he always treated me like I was his little sister. To this day I still look up to him and thank him so much for being a wonderful role model and supportive to me. He and I lost contact from the time I was eight when my mother along with two siblings moved to North Carolina from Maryland. My grandmother passed away on February 19, 1987 so from that point on, a lot of things took a turn for the worse. She held the family down and most importantly, she kept us together showing us what family love is all about. Many grandparents take on major responsibilities by raising their children's children; I still see this occurring today. After my grandmother passed away I

Chenelle M. Wiles

think there were a lot of family members who felt lost. My mother and her older sister which of course are both of my grandmother's children, were close to her and counted on my grandmother a lot. Things were vague from the time my grandmother passed in 1987 up until the time we moved to North Carolina in 1989. My mother, older brother, sister, and I moved around quite a bit. I still look back on the situations that took place in my life when I was younger and can't understand why struggles occur, but I do know that struggles are a part of life and they will either break or make us. One of my pet peeves is when people take things for granted, especially life. I remember riding in the car to various places as a child and I would see homeless people on the streets holding up "Will work for food/money" signs. I felt sorry for a lot of those people because they were hungry and didn't have places to live. Now as an adult I see firsthand how some people take advantage of standing out on the roads holding signs. I've come in contact with some so called homeless individuals that would go and purchase cigarettes and alcohol with money that people gave them. Then we have people in this society that bite the hands that feed them. I've worked with younger people for a long time even before I was an adult, and I've seen so many adolescents disrespect their parents and guardians. From cursing at the caretakers to physically hurting them, I've seen it all. True there are parents and guardians that mistreat their children and I have no tolerance for mistreatment whatsoever. Then in fact we have adults in this world that just don't have the parental skills to

Growing Up

take care of children. Those individuals try very hard to be their children's friend instead of the parent they're supposed to be. Even though my mother was very stern towards raising me, she kept the boundaries of being a parent very concrete and consistent. Being the oldest daughter of six children, a lot of things seemed unfair and a lot of responsibilities were left on me even though I wasn't the oldest. I feel as though any situation that's handed to us, we will learn from it even though it might not be a lesson until years down the road. I can remember talking to my father on the phone from time to time as a child and I could never understand why he wasn't with my older brother and me, when we relocated to North Carolina. Later on in my adult years I finally had the courage to ask my father why he didn't travel from Maryland to North Carolina to see his two children and spend more time with us. The conversation was very eye opening for my father as I expressed this to him during our talk. He didn't realize that all of those years I was missing out on a lot of things from emotional stability, to not having someone there to comfort me when I felt as though I was at a lost end in life. I think my brother who is eighteen months older than I, handled my father's absence differently. Sons connect with their mothers at a closer level than fathers do with their sons, in most cases. My mother and older brother have always been close and shared a tight bond; to this day their relationship is just as tight. So I guess my brother really didn't miss out on much, even though we did seldom talk to our father and we saw him a few times out of the years when we traveled back to

Chenelle M. Wiles

Maryland. I on the other hand didn't have that close relationship with my mother, we weren't close at all. I felt as if I was getting the raw deal, having to always care for my younger three siblings. I certainly made the best out of my times I had with my little sisters and little brother. I cherish the moments I would play house with my younger two sisters, those memories hold on to me to this very day. The oldest sibling out of the younger three is my sister (Nise) that's ten years younger than me; she is very outspoken and always has been! I can recall the days when we were younger she would wake up early in the morning making loud noises and talking, so others in the house would wake up. I would of course be a little upset because it would be a Saturday and she'd interrupt my sleep, but I would get up. I guess I didn't mind hearing her wild imaginative stories. One other sister (Netra) is eleven years younger and she's also seventeen months younger than Nise; everyone always thought they were twins when they were younger. She's my youngest sister; always been smart, quiet, and never really said much. She stayed close to me rather than talking a lot and coming up with various games to play. The youngest of all of us (S. Gordon) which is thirteen years younger than me, was the rowdy one of the clan. He was so intelligent but yet, was a riot to himself. Whenever he couldn't get his way he would fall out and have a temper tantrum, majority of the time he'd bang his head on the floor. We had family functions such as Family Reunions and he would get upset then fall out, and he would have all of us laughing so hard at him due to his ability

Growing Up

to be an actor at such a young age. I was the closest to the sister three years younger than me, when I was eighteen all the way up until the age of twenty-three we were close. We talked about a lot and even though I moved to Greensboro North Carolina which was an hour away to attend college, we stayed in touch and always talked on the phone. Most of the times when I would travel back to Charlotte to spend time with my younger three siblings, my sister and her son (my nephew) would be with us. The connection I had with my younger three siblings growing up, I kept that even when I became a young adult. I've learned that even though I help a lot of people, some people just don't have the same helping spirit in return. Even family can take advantage of an individual's generosity. I tend to look at life and the people in it in a whole different perspective. No matter how hard we push ourselves to help others, some people just don't take in the fact that they need to help themselves before they can expect others to help them. My maternal grandfather is the rock of the Howard family. When we moved to North Carolina he always came to visit us, purchased furniture for us, and got us the basic food and clothing supplies that our mother couldn't afford. No matter what we went through my grandfather usually came through when we needed him. I don't know why my grandparents split up; sometimes I just don't ask certain questions because I feel as though they're not for me to know. I never even felt the need to know why my parents didn't stay together, from what I could remember it was best due to the situations that occurred between the two of them.

Chenelle M. Wiles

I remember my father usually being affectionate whenever I saw him; giving numerous hugs and kisses. My father was adopted by my grandparents (both are now deceased) at birth. He told me when I was younger that he didn't wish to know who his biological parents were. I let him know that it was important to know due to hereditary reasons, but it was his choice and I respected that.

Elementary was kind of weird for me, my first five and a half years of grade school were completed in Maryland. I certainly don't remember any of my teachers but I recall attending a Daycare Center and a home Daycare (which was up the street from my maternal grandmother's house). My babysitter at the time was an older woman who had children and grandchildren of her own. I recall often going to her house; I even remember eating dirt one afternoon when I was playing with other children. One particular time when I traveled back to Maryland to visit my family my father and I went to see my former childhood babysitter, she still lived in the same house and she looked the same as I remembered her.

When I moved to Charlotte North Carolina in 1989, things were rough for a while. My mother, older brother, sister, and I all stayed in a shelter for a short while. I didn't understand everything that was going on and still don't today, but I do know that my mother went through a lot. My mother was coping with the death of her mother, so this was a fresh start

Growing Up

for her. Eventually we moved to an apartment on the west side of Charlotte; which was a small duplex and we attended an elementary school close by. At the time I was in the fourth grade, my older brother was also in the fourth grade, and my sister was in the first grade. My brother and I were in the same grades all throughout grade school because he was held back in one of his elementary grades. We moved to another duplex a few months later, and then my sister which is ten years younger than me was born in 1990. Sometime in 1991 my mother and her four children (including me), moved into a Housing Authority Development (Boulevard Homes) located in another area in Charlotte. In September of that same year my youngest sister was born, and the family extended to five children. I was shy and timid as a young girl and a lot of people that are close to me still can't believe it, but I knew I would make something out of my life I just didn't know when that would take place. The first two or so years living in the projects seemed to be good at times and other times things weren't so good. I felt like I didn't fit in much, I was teased a lot by a lot of people. I can remember being called "nappy head" and other cruel names. My mother didn't have much money to constantly do a lot of things for us; although I was very offended and embarrassed by the cruel things other kids said to me, I didn't complain much. I kept a lot of things to myself too and I didn't feel as though I had anyone to confide in or lean on. I had a few diaries that I continuously wrote in when I was a teenager; those diaries were misplaced when my family had to relocate to another home after I graduated from High School and headed to college. I recall documenting so much information relating to my feelings and the things I went through as a child. Living in the projects might have people thinking I grew up in a terrible neighborhood, but it wasn't a bad place! There was only one terrible incident which I can recall that occurred there. On October 5, 1993 a man was stopped by Officers John Burnette and Andy Nobles either in the neighborhood or very close to it. A chase began, involving the two police officers and that one man; both police officers were shot and killed by the man. Both of them often served in our community helping young children like myself. My household attended a local church that was approximately two to three miles from our neighborhood. Even after my mother stopped attending the church every Sunday, my younger siblings and I continued to go. I took my two youngest sisters to church and my sister which is three years younger than me, continued to go as well. The last of my mother's six children was my brother who was born on October 9, 1993. I can recall my mother going to the hospital right around the time when the two police officers were killed. A few months after the senseless killings of the officers in the neighborhood, I met this wonderful lady that started attending my church. She would talk to me during and after service sometimes, but I wasn't too quick to communicate with her. I soon found out that she was the mother of one of the officers, Officer John Burnette. It took me a while but I eventually started communicating with her. I started attending functions that she held and participated in,

Growing Up

in honor of her son and the other officer. To this very day we're still close and in touch with one another. It was a true blessing to have met her; she's had a very positive impact on my life. Her son and I also share the same birthday, which is just another blessing and she always told me that it was a reason God placed us in one another's lives. There have been a few people who have been there for me; I thank one man in particular for his kind and giving spirit. This particular man was the van driver of the church, and for many years he drove the van on many routes to various neighborhoods for people to attend church. He took a lot of children including myself under his wing and spent time with us. He would take us out to eat after church, baseball games, and just spent time with us in general.

My last grade of elementary school in which I was in the sixth grade, was very interesting. I've always been a smart young girl but I admit I didn't always utilize my intelligence to the best of my ability. Towards the end of my sixth grade, a new teacher came on board at the elementary school. She was fresh out of college from N.C. A&T S.U. in Greensboro North Carolina. She came to the school at the end of the 1991-1992 school year. She was given a group of kids that needed extra attention in various educational areas, and taught us for the remainder of the school year. I was one of the students that she had in her class; she was assigned only a few students. I started to feel as though she was just the person I needed in my life; she was patient, respectful,

Chenelle M. Wiles

energetic, and welcoming to basically all of the students in the school. At times she was treated badly by a few students, but for some reason she didn't give up on any of us. I remember the end of the year Field Day event that took place then, which was close to the last few days of school. All of the teachers and students participated in Field Day and it was so much fun! When the school year ended I knew things wouldn't be the same. Who would I talk to when I needed someone to? Who would help me get through the day when all I could think about was other children were teasing me? Well it wasn't her because I was no longer going to that school where she was teaching. I still remember the last day of school, leaving to go home on the school bus and all of us children were waving goodbye to the teachers. The last person I remember seeing was that teacher and I waved until I couldn't see her any longer.

Well, Junior High arrived and I was in the seventh grade. Not too long after school started I did a lot of thinking about how well things went for me towards the end of elementary, when that one teacher came to my school. I was at a different school but still had other children tease me about my appearance, mostly my hair. So one day I took it upon myself to go talk to my seventh grade guidance counselor. I can't recall the specific conversation but to sum it up the best way I can: I asked her was there any way she could get in touch with the teacher who taught me last year, Miss Turner at the time? I expressed to my guidance counselor that I really

Growing Up

wanted to talk to her, and I was hoping she still taught at the elementary school which was right beside the junior high school I was attending. Three schools were right beside one another the elementary, junior high, and high school. My guidance counselor let me know she was going to help me, but it would take a few days. I was called to the office one day during one of my classes about a week later, and I was very surprised when I walked into my guidance counselor's office. There was Miss Turner the same teacher that taught me at the end of my sixth grade year, sitting in my guidance counselor's office. I got to talk to her for a while, and I was probably one of the happiest people in the school that particular day!

As I continued to advance in school grade by grade, I had her with me in my life. Although I didn't see her a lot during the following two years or so, she and I communicated on the phone and she would often come to see me at my home and school. All of this time I was still residing in the projects in Charlotte, with my mother and five other siblings. I got involved in a summer camp program through my church when I was about fourteen or fifteen. My sister that's three years younger than me was also in that summer camp program. We did various activities relating to self-esteem, peer relationships, sex, abuse, education, respect, and so much more. We went on trips a few times out of the week

Chenelle M. Wiles

and even went to the beach. I enjoyed most of my peers that attended that camp; I guess we shared common interests. I joined the junior high school track team when I was in the eighth grade, even though I wasn't very fast I still enjoyed the event I participated in which were the hurdles. I also went out for basketball in the eighth grade but I didn't make the team, I made it to the last cut which was a surprise to me. Junior High was an experience, it had its ups and downs and that made me move forward and work harder.

When high school came along, then came three years of the best years of my life, but of course they came with some disappointments as well. Here I was fresh out of junior high, going into the tenth grade of high school. I was even more involved in church; I helped put on puppet shows for the Sunday School Classes and I enjoyed that a lot. I can remember doing funny voices for the different characters I portrayed in the bible for our presentations to the younger children. Tenth grade was also the year I seemed to develop a terrible attitude problem. The one and only time I got suspended from school was my tenth grade year. I don't recall the exact events but I caught an attitude with my social studies teacher, and was sent to the office. I got in trouble at home by my mother, but that was a consequence that followed my negative action. Probably in the middle of the

Growing Up

school year I started spending time with Miss Turner. She'd pick me up and we would go different places. She would always talk to me and encourage me to do my best in school, and to stay out of trouble. She actually took me on my first visit to get my hair professionally done at a salon. I was in the tenth grade at that time and most girls were getting their hair professionally done in junior high. Well after that first visit, I was going to the salon on a regular basis to get my hair done, I got my hair cut short and shaved in the back. It was a new me starting off with my appearance. The summer before my eleventh grade year of high school, I did a lot of things. I went to Maryland to spend time with my family for a few weeks. I spent time with my former and favorite teacher that I ever had, Miss Turner of course. The peers I used to hang out with in my neighborhood, I didn't really hang out with them anymore. I got my first job during my junior year of high school; I worked at an athletic club in downtown Charlotte. I enjoyed that job a lot, one of my best friends at the time worked there as well. My other best friend was pregnant at the time and had a baby our senior year in high school, in which her daughter was my Godchild. I got my driver's license when I was in the eleventh grade, and that was an accomplishment in itself because I was one of the few teenagers who had their license in the area in which I lived. It was weird because my mother took my older brother and I to get our license at the same time, I passed mine and received my license but he didn't. My brother did in fact get his driver's license when he got a little older. Thank God I got my license because I previously totaled my mother's car when I took my three younger siblings and the son of the boyfriend that my mother was dating at the time, to the mall. I also ran over my former teacher's (Miss Turner) mailbox; we were heading to the amusement park in Charlotte and I was driving her car, I backed down her driveway which was on a hill, without stopping. Those were some embarrassing times but very valuable and important lessons that I learned to overcome in my life. At home things were alright, I was still babysitting my younger three siblings but not as much as I had to when I was younger. When I was in the eleventh grade one of my two younger sisters was in the first grade, my youngest sister was in the kindergarten, and my little brother was three and in Daycare. I went to the prom my junior year with a senior, he was very attractive and a gentleman. I asked him to the prom instead of him asking me, that's a shock to me now because I didn't think I was pretty enough to go out with guys who were as attractive as he was. My former favorite teacher took me shopping for a prom dress, and all of the other things that went along with going to the prom. As I started spending more time with her, we considered each other to be family and we called one another God sisters.

 As I gained a God sister, I began to see how it was to have an older sister to count on instead of always having people count on me. I met her family and spent a lot of time with

Growing Up

them as well. At the time she had a sister that was a senior in college at her alma mater, N.C. A&T S.U. in Greensboro North Carolina. During the same year I went on my first college tour to that particular school, her sister graduated from there (in 1997). I attended her graduation with all of her family; all of them took me in as family and I felt so welcome. Her sister also became my God sister; all three of us began spending time together every once in a while.

 I was excited going into my senior year of high school! I wasn't going to be going to the same high school that I had been going to; I was going to a different high school on another side of town. My oldest God sister was the dance team coach and my other God sister was the cheerleading coach at this school. The high school that I attended my tenth and eleventh grade years was a good high school and it was the school I was assigned to attend due to the neighborhood I was living in. I started to explore different things so I took my God sister's advice and went to a different school my last year of high school; this particular school seemed to be one of the most popular ones! Even though I was a new student at this high school, I felt very comfortable because I spent a lot of time with a few other students that had already been attending the school. I became the manager of the dance team during my senior year. The summer before my senior year I attended camps with my God sister and her dance girls; helping them out with different things for the camps. I met some wonderful people and we all became good friends for the entire school year. They performed half time shows during all of the school's Friday night football games; they performed with the school's Marching Band! Being involved with an activity such as that was a wonderful experience because I enjoyed helping people, but this time I was helping people that were my age. I also enjoyed hanging with them outside of school activities; some of the girls would often hang out at my God sister's house! I was hardly at home in my neighborhood anymore due to the time I put in helping my God sister and my friends that were dance girls. I had a lot of fun with my new group of friends! I recall a time when the dance team were practicing for our Homecoming show: We were all clowning around after they got new sweat suits with their names inscribed on them for the Homecoming show. One of the dancers was driving down to the football field from the band room, so a few of us decided to get on the hood and trunk of the car to ride down to the field. Well that was obviously a foolish idea, but of course that's some of the things that teenagers decide to do. The girl that was driving the car increased her speed just a little too much and that caused most of us to fall off of the car onto the pavement. I was one of the ones who fell off of the car and I ended up being the only one who got injured. I was on the trunk of the car and when she increased her speed I fell and ended up busting the back of my head. Blood was everywhere and I had to be taken to the emergency room. I had to get a few stitches in the back of my head and both of my God sisters were at the

Growing Up

hospital with me. My oldest God sister witnessed the entire incident and felt responsible because she didn't do anything to prevent it, but accidents happen, and besides it was her car in which the accident occurred. After that incident happened we all joked about it and thought how crazy we were for doing something like that. My twelfth grade year of high school was probably the best year of school for me. I went to my senior prom with one of my best friends and we had a good time with the people we went with. I was still working on weekends and some days after school, at the athletic club. When I graduated from high school in 1998, I not only knew that I was going to be successful but I was ready to begin the next chapter in my life. After graduation I went to Myrtle Beach in South Carolina for a week with both of my God sisters and a lot of members of the dance and cheerleading teams; which was a wonderful and rewarding vacation for all of us! Besides attending camps, I've never been able to get away with people my age so that was new for me. After that vacation I went back to Charlotte and lived with my oldest God sister for the summer; my mother was no longer living in our neighborhood in which we grew up in due to financial issues. We had been residing in that housing authority development for seven years, and it was one of the most stable places we've lived in. Not too long after returning to Charlotte from the beach, I went to Maryland for a few weeks to spend time with my family for part of the summer. On July 6, 1998 I found out I was accepted to N.C. A&T S.U.; my God sister had

Chenelle M. Wiles

called me from Charlotte to my aunt and uncle's house in Maryland where I was visiting at the time, to deliver the news. Everyone was so excited and I was very excited myself, to be one of the first to attend college out of my family.

From birth up until the age of seventeen when I graduated from high school, a lot had taken place in my life. I went through difficult times, endured a lot of mental, emotional, and even physical pain, and I also grew up fast while I was a child due to the responsibilities I upheld. Although hardships took place, I was very blessed. My mother instilled values in me that I needed to follow rules in life and be responsible. I fully understood that but I didn't understand why I was one of the only children who had to do so much, follow strict guidelines, and in return not be appreciated. I lost my grandmother when I was about six years old, but I kept her memory and love she had for me, deep within me. It amazes a lot of people in my family of how well my memory is of my grandmother, due to the fact that she passed away when I was very young. I struggled early on in my years of school but I stayed on top of my education; as I got older I earned a scholarship from the high school I attended during my senior year titled "The Lion Heart Award!" That award went with me when I entered my freshman year of college at A&T in August of 1998, as I started off studying Nursing. I was going to be leaving my younger siblings and honestly they were who I worried about the most, but I knew I had to make a life

Growing Up

for myself, so college was where it was starting.

Before I officially became an adult which was at the age of eighteen, I'd accomplished the simple life skill of overcoming adversities. No matter what it took, I wasn't going to be subjected to fall into the statistics in which I grew up in. Having true people in my life pays off but no matter what I went through, my back bone was the strongest for me in my years of growing up. One of my older cousins (Stephanie) on my maternal side of the family, always told me not to worry about things when crazy stuff would occur at our Family Reunions or family get togethers. She still has awesome talks with me to this very day even though we live in two separate cities. People can be legally grown but certain actions we take may not add up to us being grown. I not only encourage myself to continue to grow in life by keeping my faith in my higher power, but I put myself first in decisions I make in my life now. I grew up always putting myself last and helping others without thinking of my well-being, but as I consistently did that most of the people I helped either walked over me or wasn't willing to take care of me when I was at my worse. It's totally fine to put yourself first; we can't help others unless we know how to help ourselves first. I was told by various people who genuinely cared for me that I needed to step back from giving to others so much and I needed to give more to myself. Well I heard that a lot but I didn't start implementing the advice I was given until I was about twenty-seven. The saying "Better late than never" applied to me at that point in my life due to me losing out on self-happiness for so long. I didn't care to set aside the feelings for myself; I gave so much of myself, to others. Even though I wasn't willing to do so at the time, I've grown mentally, physically, emotionally, and spiritually.

In 1995 before my sophomore year of high school, I was selected to attend a camp called Camp Anytown. Camp Anytown is a nationally recognized and award winning diversity, leadership, and social justice program for youth ages 15-18. For one week I attended the camp with other high school students, utilizing our positive strengths even though we were all from different communities and backgrounds. I became comfortable with my peers during that week. I remember coming up with a step with a few other teenagers and we put on a wonderful performance for one of the talent shows. A few years during my senior year, later I attended the same high school with some of the teenagers that attended Camp Anytown with me.

Growing up is a part of life, the only thing promised in life is death. We should never forget what growing up brought us into, when it relates to our present life. On the other hand we shouldn't dwell on our rough times; they should only make us stronger. There are a lot of tasks I didn't complete to the best of my ability, but I'm pleased with how I overcame adversities and made something positive out of my life. We all have a calling in life; my calling has always been to help others when they needed help with many things, specifically younger people. Sometimes we never know why certain things happen, but that's just the way life is. I guess the reason why I was gifted to help younger people was because I started out helping my younger siblings on a consistent basis. Even though I didn't have someone who was consistently there for me when I was younger, I made a way for me to be there for other people that needed someone and that stayed within me throughout life.

Now that I'm grown and have been for a while, I not only help younger people, I help those who are the same age and older than me. I look at different situations in different perspectives; everyone needs help every now and then but we have to help ourselves first. We have to give ourselves a chance to grow and do what's necessary to make something out of our lives in the best way possible. I'm an adult but I'm still growing in every way that I can imagine such as mentally, emotionally, and even spiritually. So I encourage everyone to grow to the level of potential in which they were created to be on.

2. Giving Back

Accomplishments happen a lot in a lifetime, some people find accomplishments easily rewarding and others might find them to be very difficult. Whatever the difference may be, accomplishments often make us want to continue achieving them. When I was younger I didn't think I'd reach any of my goals but no matter how hard I was on myself, I'm an accomplishment today simply by being blessed to be a mentor to others.

Wikipedia defines mentor as a trusted friend, counselor, or teacher, usually a more experienced person. I had a few people who were influential to me in my life as I was growing up; they certainly were and still are mentors to me. We can all learn the simplest things in life from others who may rarely be around us. True indeed as we're young, we all pick habits from others that are negative and we even pass them on to others. In the same sense, we have to discipline ourselves to make sound decisions either to do what's right or what's wrong. Being a mentor shouldn't be just something we do for recognition, we should step in and help others because it comes natural. Helping could be a need or a want; most of my life I felt as if I needed to help others. In my life now, I help others because I want to. I strongly feel that giving back is something I need to do, but if I can't put myself first then helping others can't happen.

Starting at the age of eighteen, I began to mentor others. It was a month after I entered my freshman year of college that

Chenelle M. Wiles

I took on the role of being a mentor. I landed a job at a local YMCA as an afterschool counselor, right beside the dormitory I was residing in. I worked a few days after my classes from two until six in the afternoons. It was a great part time job that I could do what I loved, which was help younger people. Being a college student and not having much money was an issue, so having some spending money had me feel a little more independent. Not having to worry about where my extra expenses were going to come from relieved a little stress as well.

At that time I was primarily working with five and six year olds, which were kindergarten and first graders. I was assigned to this particular group of children with one other counselor. Young children have so much energy, it's like they never stop moving. We had a schedule we had to follow of course; when they arrived at the YMCA after they got out of school they were given snacks after their bathroom break. Then they had homework time, so for thirty minutes, time was set aside for them to complete homework or read a book; most of the time my partner and I would read to them. Those young children brought a lot of creativity out of me. We put on talent and fashion shows, played a lot of competitive games, and even let them act as if they were counselors from time to time.

Things were running smooth for me at the YMCA. I started having other children that were older than the ones in my group, come to my class. Sometimes I had teenagers that attended the afterschool program, come and read to my five and six year olds. Then other times I'd get some of the children that had disciplinary problems come to my group and help out, I guess I was the "time out" counselor. I really didn't understand why some children were sent to my class, all of the children for the most part loved my class. It was alright though, because I put them to work either by assisting me or having them write about what they did and how they could prevent it from happening in the future. I recall one incident in which a parent didn't appreciate the fact that I had her son who was probably eight at the time, write a short paragraph about respecting others. When she picked her children up that afternoon, she noticed that one of her children was in my class writing, she walked through the other door and slung it open really hard. She then went to complain to my supervisor that I shouldn't have had her son write a paper. My supervisor talked to me and in so many words she told me that I should've just had him sit aside in time out for about ten minutes. I guess some methods of discipline are just misunderstood.

Within the first year of working at the YMCA, I had two teenage girls who were about thirteen, always come to either my class or to me in passing through the halls. They simply would speak to me and tell me how their day went. They really were special and they obviously saw something in me that they needed; that's my assumption. After communicating with them a lot during the afterschool program, we all talked about me being their mentor. They were best friends even though they went to different middle schools; they met each other in the afterschool program at the YMCA. After talking to their mothers about me being their mentor, things began to be solid and I became something like a big sister to both of them. I made sure they were doing their homework at the YMCA after school, staying on top of their personal responsibilities, and talking to them about their concerns and other things that were often on their mind. I still remain close to them to this day and we communicate periodically, even talking about the days when we were all at the YMCA.

When I was entering my senior year of high school I was given a nickname. One of the dance girls on my God sister's team as well as my other God sister's (Tasha) husband, gave me the nickname CoCo. That name seemed to be my name starting at that point in time; hardly anyone outside of my immediate family called me Chenelle any longer. When I started working at the "Y" all of my coworkers and children there called me "Miss CoCo." It was kind of weird being called my nickname at my workplace and on top of that having the Miss title in front of it, but a lot of staff members were called by their nicknames. I was very comfortable with the children, my coworkers, and even the parents calling me Miss CoCo.

Giving Back

Being a mentor seemed to be a great way to give back. Even though the two mentees I had at that time both had loving parents that were supportive and structured, I was like an older sister to them that they didn't have. Both of the girls were the oldest out of their parent's children, so they had to be the role models for their younger sisters. I had four younger siblings and didn't have older siblings so all three of us related to one another in that sense. I began to mentor many more youth than I expected to; a lot of times children just need to know that someone outside of their family cares for them.

I really started using my talents to the best of my ability, as I continued to work at the YMCA. How ironic, my God sister that taught me in elementary worked at that same "Y" when she attended A&T, so years later I was working at that very same place. I started a dance and step class for boys and girls; we often put on performances for their parents, staff, other members of the "Y," and their families throughout different times of the year. As time went on my groups performed in the N.C. A&T S.U. Homecoming Parades, Daycare Graduations, and so many other events. This was another passion in life that I gained and loved, and I continued to keep the youth busy and give them a chance to put their talents on display for others to see.

Chenelle M. Wiles

I was never on a school basketball team when I was growing up but was on one team for teenagers through one of the programs I was in, and I recall us competing one time at a local college in Charlotte. I decided to coach basketball not too long after working at the "Y," as well as start up my dance and step teams. The YMCA had seasonal basketball leagues your youth, so I decided to coach. I started out coaching a coed five and six year old team. That team consisted of nine or ten players and both of my mentee's brothers played on my teams. My first group of players showed me that no matter if they had the skills or not, they could play as a team. One team went undefeated with a record of 10-0; that was the first season I was a Basketball Coach. I continued to coach a team of four and five year olds for about a year after that, and I enjoyed it a lot. I coached all throughout the year, coaching all ages from five all the way up to thirteen. I also was an assistant coach for a female Amateur Athletic Union team for ages twelve and under. AAU teams compete and travel against other teams, it's rewarding and can take up a lot of time. I only stayed with the AAU team for one season, it was rewarding but my weekends were dedicated to traveling and coaching basketball games which I didn't enjoy that for too long. Coach CoCo took a rest from coaching basketball, although I still attended basketball games that my former players were playing for on either their school, AAU, or other teams. I then stopped coaching basketball at the "Y", even though I loved coaching I just needed some "me" time.

Giving Back

Camps are fun and sometimes give us lifetime experiences that we share with others and through various situations that come in our lives. Who would've known that one of the same camps I attended when I was younger, would be the same camp I'd chaperone other teenagers in my adult years. I attended this camp called Camp Thunderbird which wasn't too far from Charlotte NC. It was an overnight camp and it probably lasted a few days; we did a lot of activities and stayed in cabins. Years later when I was a young adult, I was a chaperone at that same camp. The camp made a few changes, it later became a Christian Camp. I actually chaperoned at the camp twice; a few of the teenagers from the YMCA that I worked at, attended the camp. I later ran into some of the young adults that attended the camp when I was a chaperone and when they were the campers. It's so rewarding to see them as adults; most of them were being role models as adults to other children in similar positions they were in when they were children.

Another wonderful camp I attended when I was about fifteen years old was Camp Anytown. A lot of different teachers and counselors saw positive things in me that I didn't see in myself so they recommended for me to attend the camp. Camp Anytown is an intensive four day, three night residential leadership development retreat. It's a nationally recognized and award winning diversity, leadership, and social justice program for youth ages 15-18. I did things at

Chenelle M. Wiles

Camp Anytown that I never thought I'd do. I was involved in a step performance with a few other teenagers, and we all put on a wonderful Step Show performance for the camp. I met some unique and gifted people that were chaperones; they genuinely cared and loved all the campers such as myself. I met a few teenagers there that I later saw when I attended the same school they were attending, which was the high school I attended for one year in Charlotte North Carolina. The times I did get out of my neighborhood and into productive and constructive things were when I attended camps such as Camp Thunderbird and Camp Anytown. I thank my mother for allowing me to attend those camps as well as my teachers, counselors, and other adults for recommending me to experience life skills that I needed. Camps aren't just getaways where people can enjoy time away from their regular life, but the experience can be life changing and influential in a major way. I encourage every adolescent to experience some time at a camp, not just any camp but a camp designed to reach certain people in areas in which they'd benefit from in life.

    Growing up I would see certain actors, actresses, singers, and other entertainers and I would want to be like them. In a lot of adolescent's eyes, the flashy cars, jewelry, and other glamorous items are the perfect things to a wonderful life. What I didn't realize and a lot of other teenagers as well, were that material things won't serve as total happiness in our lives. Certain jobs that people get in their lives, the

Giving Back

money often tends to be a major distraction and the job itself isn't interesting. I was always told by different people that we can make a lot of money but not enjoy our job that pays us plenty of money. I learned a lot about giving back by working at the YMCA when I moved to Greensboro North Carolina. I wasn't making much money at all when I was employed at the "Y", but the experience had a positive impact on my life while I was there and it reflects on me to this very day in my life. All of the extra things I did outside of just working at the YMCA, I enjoyed them and did it from the heart.

If I had the mentality as a younger person that I have now as an adult, I would've been more willing to accept myself as I was and not worry about the fame that I was seeing in others. Growing is a part of life whether we want to accept it or not, it will happen as long as we have life. Being an adult has advantages and disadvantages and being a child also have its advantages and disadvantages. Children generally don't have to worry about bills, reporting to jobs, and financially taking care of others. I've heard stories of my ancestors having to work when they were very young to help pay bills. In the generation in which I grew up in I didn't have to do those things, and I was and still am very grateful for that. Adults have to take care of numerous financial responsibilities, as well as taking care of themselves and possibly any dependents. There are many parents who choose not to take care of their responsibilities then there are many who aren't able to take care of their responsibilities due to things that

Chenelle M. Wiles

have happened in their lives.

Giving may be something that we often feel like we must do and on the other hand, giving could be something that we just want to do. When we make the choice to have children, I feel as if giving love, support, and basic needs are all things we have to do. Some people give naturally and willingly, it seems as if it's something they were born to do. I've gone without plenty of things in my life as a child such as places to live, electricity, running water, food, and even family. Many people go without so much in life every day and most of those people are able and willing to remain humble and not lose their personal faith. I admit that there have been plenty of times in my life in which I've been down and I lost my hope and faith. Even though I often felt like I was down, I've never been out because if I was out, then I would've given up on myself. Giving up on myself was something I obviously didn't do because I'm still working hard and doing things I never imagined to do, at this very point in my life. It's a saying that I've heard so many times in my life and it states "You can't help everyone but you can start out helping others one person at a time." That statement holds a lot of truth; I wanted to help so many people but some didn't want to be helped then at other times when I wanted to help others, I simply didn't have the certain tools to provide the help they needed.

We've all heard the basic saying "It's better to give then to receive." I try to put that saying in a lot of things I do with my

Giving Back

life, but it's easier said than done. If we come in contact with people that are in need and they may come across as being rude, disrespectful, or whatever the case, we might be reluctant to give them things they might need. No matter how things come at us, it's not up to us to punish people that come at us the way we don't want them to, when they're in need. I admit I've refused to help some people that were rude and did things that weren't right to me, when they really needed help in the end. Thinking about ourselves is very important and we should take good care of ourselves mentally, physically, and emotionally. How can we as individuals help others if we're failing to take care of ourselves first and foremost? I've been given advice so many times from some very important people in my life, regarding me going above and beyond to help people that didn't or don't want to help themselves. My immediate family has been through a lot of difficult times when I was coming up as a child. When I left home for college, my mother was still raising four children on her own. I wasn't going to be around to help my siblings like I've always been but I knew I had to move on and live my life. My mother wasn't and will never be perfect and nobody will, but she did more for her six children then our fathers ever did and that was being a full time parent. When I left my siblings to go to college, I knew I had to help myself so that I could help them better in the long run with finances and by basically making something out of my life, so they could follow in my positive steps.

After I continued to work at the "Y" I stepped up and was a mentor to a lot of children. A few children that often got into trouble at school and in the home, their parents would explain their situations to me. I took it upon myself to talk to them about the decisions they were making and sometimes it would help, but other times it wouldn't. As time went on I was no longer working at the YMCA but I remained close to a lot of different families of the children that attended the "Y." I often went to some of the schools where the children went and ate lunch with them, volunteered at field day events, chaperoned field trips, and a lot of other helpful things. I became friends with a few parents of the children, and they were all older than me so I not only learned things from them but they saw how I was working with their children and learned a lot from me as well. Parents called me and talked about things that were going on with them and their families, and I even attended family functions with them. I guess I had a few families that looked at me as I was their family, and I saw it that way as well. Most of the younger males I worked with often struggled in school and exhibited behavioral issues. Now those males are mostly in college and doing great things with their lives. Other young males made decisions to not do so well in life and they're incarcerated. There are some young males I've worked with that either played basketball on one of my teams when I coached, were in a group home, or attended the YMCA which communicated with me by writing me from the facility in which they were incarcerated. Most times I found out that certain youngsters

Giving Back

were incarcerated so I extended letters to them, to basically encourage them to do what it takes to get their lives on the right track. Most of the females I've worked with didn't present the same problems as the males did in their future. Now a few females have fallen below their own expectations and fell off the right track, but for the most part the females have done well with themselves. I've worked with a lot of young ladies who had children when they were teenagers, but most of them have been doing great jobs as mothers. I've gone to see some of the young ladies after they've given birth to their children and have been invited to various events for their children.

It feels good to hear success stories about the young people I've worked with. I've been out and about numerous times and I would often get stopped by parents of the children I've worked with in the past. The parents would ask "Didn't you work with my child when they were younger?" Sometimes I wouldn't recognize who they were, but they would feel me in on how their child was doing and other times they'd thank me for being there for their child. Experiences like that are what make the smaller things in life worthwhile. I never help people to get recognized, I do it because I know it's the right thing to do! When I was younger I had some wonderful people come in my life to help me and they're still in my life, so I know how it feels to have someone there for you! It amazes me how the help from others pays off in the long run. This year one of my mentees graduated

Chenelle M. Wiles

from college; I've been her mentor since she was twelve. One of my younger siblings (Nise) whom moved with me her senior year of high school following her pregnancy, became friends with a lot of the young people I worked with when they were younger.

My mother had six children and as of June 2011, are all high school graduates. Even though I endured a lot of responsibilities at a very young age, it was a great feeling to witness them successfully complete high school. When my younger siblings were younger I worried sometimes like when my younger brother used to have temper tantrums in school. Then as he got older he'd get involved on sports teams and I would travel from Greensboro to Charlotte to watch his middle school football games. He also got involved in the marching band at his high school which was also the school I graduated from; I enjoyed seeing him march and perform at the Friday night football games. Then my two sisters following under me in age, were both involved in the ROTC program (one at my alma mater high school and one other one was at another high school). My sister Sheriliah, I saw a few of her competitions and appearances in parades because we went to the same high school for one year. When I was a senior in high school, she was a freshman in high school. My sister Nise whom is ten years younger than me, I chaperoned field trips for her and went to see her perform in different events with her ROTC Program. My youngest sister (Netra) wasn't involved in school activities but I still spent a lot of

Giving Back

time with her; whenever I went to Charlotte she was with me like my other siblings were. When my sister (Sheriliah) had her son when she was a teenager, I often took him places along with my younger three siblings. I enjoyed spending time with my younger siblings and showing them different things in life.

As I continued to get older I started to realize that even though I enjoyed helping and doing for others, I needed to do some things for myself. I've spent so much time out of my everyday life just giving to others but I needed to enjoy my life. A lot of times I take time out for others and they might not say they needed help, but I stepped in anyway. Prime example was when I made the decision to adopt my son back in 2006, he didn't ask to come in my life but I stepped up and did it because I wanted to help him.

Even as an adult and already living in Greensboro I went through difficult times, people stepped up and helped me out with places to stay and by talking to me when I needed someone to talk to. I went through some financial hardships and one of my roommates at one time worked with me by setting up payment arrangements when I fell short on a lot of bills. A few other people that became my friends opened up their homes to me and I lived with them for a while, I'm forever grateful for them all giving so freely to me. I have so many people that have become extended family to me, it's such a blessing and I don't take their kindness for granted.

Chenelle M. Wiles

Giving tangible things in life could often be expensive but the intangible things that are given in life, are often the greatest gifts. When we take time out to talk and listen to others, that's an intangible gift that lasts a lifetime.

   Family often expects a lot of things out of each other, whether it's helping each other or even enabling one another. I've had a lot of incidents in which I stopped helping certain family members, then I was talked about negatively. I was even compared with the way I help others that aren't in the family. As I look at those situations I tell myself I'm a grown woman and free individual, so with that said I'm allowed to help whomever I want and whenever I want. Giving is a choice and it should be done freely from the heart, not to please people. A lot of celebrities give back by spending time with people in communities, volunteering time, and even donating money to various organizations. Many celebrities and athletes have been through similar struggles in life that a lot of people like myself, have been in. So with that said they step up and do things for people that are in situations that they were once in themselves. I recall shortly after moving to North Carolina in 1989 and Hurricane Hugo hit hard in Charlotte, damaging a lot or areas. Homes and businesses were destroyed, and people lended helping hands as well as money. I recall in the past years the September 11, 2001 tragedies and even Hurricane Katrina that occurred in Louisiana, many people including celebrities helped out during those tough times.

Giving Back

I've been a member of my home church in Charlotte North Carolina since I was a teenager. The church members have helped me so much and I still keep in touch with so many of them. The same pastor that was the leader of the congregation when I was a teenager and began going to the church, still remains the leader of the church. A lot of the church family members helped me and a lot of young people get involved with church functions so we could stay out of trouble and involved with constructive activities. I had an attitude problem with a few church members when I was a teenager and I really can't explain why I did. As I got older I began to get more involved with various church functions, and that's how I became more aware that how I treated people would impact my life. I enjoyed doing things for others and with that said, helping and doing for others while having a negative attitude doesn't get anyone anywhere productive in life. Being a big part of the Sunday School Puppet Show Performances, was such a great experience for me when I was a teenager. It was something we did every Sunday for the young children in Sunday school and it gave me the chance to show my humorous side. I didn't think about anything else that was bothering me at that time because I was doing some things I really enjoyed.

One of the greatest things I think I've ever done or given was my son a mother. I adopted my son when he was thirteen and he came into my life when he was twelve.

Chenelle M. Wiles

I've always thought about adopting a child but I didn't think it would happen when I was twenty-five. It's not easy to raise a child let alone raise a child that's already set in their ways. I've witnessed my son come from a lot of struggles to push every helping hand in his path out of his way, to him being and still becoming a young man who is willing to make wiser decisions in his life. One thing my son has always been good at was helping others, he likes to keep his hands moving. He would often take things apart such as his radio or bike, and then I would laugh with him because he wouldn't put it back together. Patience is something that runs thin with a lot of people, I'm aware that I get impatient with a lot of things. I started talking to my son about doing things for others even when he first came into our home; he was very interested in helping on his own though. We volunteered at local restaurants during Thanksgiving and Christmas, to help feed the homeless. Those opportunities were priceless, I let him know that he should never take anything for granted especially life. He let me know that he enjoyed helping out with that particular event and we often helped people out different times of the year. An experience such as that one was a very important lesson and humbling experience for the both of us. Not being able to help every person that's in need that I come in contact with saddens me, but being able to help at least one person every so often makes me feel good.

3. Relationships

Relationships are a part of every human's life and they involve both good and bad ones. I know so much about relationships because they have played a big role in my life. As defined by Answers.com relationships are the ways in which two or more concepts, objects, or people are connected, or the state of being connected. Relationships deal with family, dating, friends, marriage, jobs, school, and so much more.

When I entered this world with life, I entered it alone but with the assistance of a few people. Before I entered the world I was connected closely to my mother inside of her, like all other unborn babies. As a baby I relied on my parents to mold and connect with me, that's what parents are supposed to do. The first five years of my life I was connected very closely to my maternal family. As we get older in life our memories tend to fade, especially the young and tender years of birth through age five. My older brother, sister behind me in age, and I were all brought up very closely around our maternal family. We saw our grandmother daily and even lived with her for a few years. My grandmother was raising a few of my older cousins around the time when we were always at her house before she passed, I'm so thankful for the memories I still have when she was in my life. I was six when she passed away, my brother was eight, and my sister was three. My grandmother held the family down! It seemed like her house was never empty because everyone was always

Chenelle M. Wiles

there; we had a close knit family. I can't recall the events that took place but my grandmother took my brother, a few of my cousins, and myself all to Disney World in Florida when I was about three or four. I was the youngest out of all the children that she took on that trip so I really can't remember how much fun we had, and none of my family members have any pictures from it. I heard from a few family members that we came back and talked about how much fun we all had. A lot of grandmothers and grandfathers do a lot of things to keep their families strong. Although my maternal grandparents were divorced before I entered this world, they both spent a great deal of time with their grandchildren. My mother and her oldest sister were the only two children that my grandparents shared; my mother is the only biological child of her father. My mother's father (my grandfather William) adopted her older sister when she was young. My maternal grandmother (Shirley) cared for a lot of children that weren't her own, especially in our family. Being together with family seemed to be very important to a lot of people in my family, so as a child that made me and my other family members very happy. I always saw my father even when he and my mother split up; we all lived in Maryland. A lot of family time was cut off when my lovely grandmother passed away in February of 1987. Even though I was only six, I remember a lot about her. The family basically fell apart, the person that held the family together was gone and wasn't coming back to hold us together.

Relationships

The relationship that the family shared which was being closely bonded had vanished and left like my grandmother did. We went from having a house full of grandchildren, nieces, nephews, children, and a lot of other family members, to a house that was empty. I'm still confused as to what events took place that caused not one single family member to keep my grandmother's house, but my grandmother's house soon became vacant. A lot of people disappeared and the family was a mess. I went from seeing my two older cousins every day, to not seeing them at all. My older brother, sister, and myself all went from going to our babysitter's house (which was about a block up the street from our grandmother's house) every day to not going to her house anymore. One day my mother, brother, sister, and I all went on a long road trip and who knew that particular road trip would be a new change in our lives.

Confusion followed my grandmother's death; it was painful and kept conflicts open between many family members. My mother soon took her three children from Landover Maryland to Charlotte North Carolina. She didn't tell any of our family that she was leaving and as an adult she didn't have to, but for people like my father and grandfather, I guess they needed to know where we were for our safety. My mother had to make things better for herself and her children because it was nothing less than chaos when we were in Maryland after my grandmother was gone. I can recall the trip to North Carolina, it was a long trip at that. I

Chenelle M. Wiles

still remember my mother's car which was a two door red car named Renault, whatever that was. One particular incident I can recall on our way to NC from MD was when we stopped at a rest area and somebody had a hot drink that was probably tea or coffee. It spilled on my lap when I was sitting down due to the front passenger seat hitting the drink, when my brother was getting in the car. The family oriented relationship that the four of us shared with our large family, simmered down to just a relationship between the four of us that were relocating, two states away.

When we moved to Charlotte back in 1989 we stayed in a shelter in downtown Charlotte. I'm not sure how long we resided in the shelter but I don't think it was very long. We eventually moved into an apartment and were in elementary school. At that time we relocated it was towards the end of the school year; my sister was in the first grade, and my brother and I were both in the fourth. My brother was behind one year so that's why both of us were in the same grade. We moved twice after we left the shelter and we moved around quite often when were in Maryland before we moved to Charlotte. It's an understatement to say times were difficult for my mother. I'm not sure if it was the first or second summer that we were in North Carolina but my mother's father came down from Maryland to see us, then he took us back to Maryland for some of the summer. When we went back to Maryland with our grandfather, we were only connecting with some our family members on my

Relationships

grandfather's side of the family. My grandfather had a sister that lived in Charlotte North Carolina and his mother, younger sister, and a few other family members lived in Wadesboro North Carolina. My grandfather is from Wadesboro and he's the oldest of thirteen children. The Howard's which is my grandfather's side of the family, are a large family. We began to have a relationship with the Howards; we had family reunions every other year in the summer time. My maternal grandparents both had and still have strong families and throughout my early, middle, and teenage childhood years I spent a lot of time with both sides. I lost contact with my grandmother's side of the family for years after moving to North Carolina. I thought about one cousin in particular on my grandmother's side which was my older cousin Troy. He is eight years older than me and is my grandmother's brother's son. His mother passed away as a result of a car accident when he was a young child, so my grandmother raised him. He called my grandmother "grandma" even though she's his aunt. He seemed like a big brother to me but that relationship faded for a long time after moving away to NC. Twenty something years later, I got in touch with him and we talked on the phone for about an hour our first talk. My mother had been communicating with him and they're first cousins. My mother then gave my contact information to him so that he could call me. We finally spoke to one another on the phone and it was a good feeling for me, I couldn't remember how he looked because we'd been gone for so long, but I felt comfortable talking to the cousin I remember being around for a while when I was younger. From that moment and then on, we kept in contact and I saw him from time to time when I traveled back to Maryland to visit my family.

I'm not quite sure how often my mother communicated with her family on her mother and father's side after we relocated, but I didn't communicate with anyone in Maryland from my family but a select few when I was a child. There was a period of time in which we didn't have a telephone when we moved to NC so we used a pay phone to communicate with our grandfather, me and my brother's father, an aunt and uncle, and my Godmother. From 1989 up until the time I started driving on my own which was in 1996, my other took us to Maryland at least once a year on one of the major holidays, and other times my grandfather would come to get us for summer vacations. I really enjoyed seeing my family, we always went to my grandfather's house. My grandfather had remarried when I was young and it was when my grandmother was still living. His wife has a son which is my uncle by marriage, by his mother and my grandfather. My uncle and his wife, along with their two children, were family whom we saw and spent a lot of time with whenever we went back to Maryland. My mother really didn't care too much for my grandfather's wife; they hardly spoke to one another or carried lengthy conversations at all. As I got a little older I didn't know why but I felt as though I couldn't hold many conversations with my grandfather's wife either; in a

Relationships

way I didn't think she treated me and my siblings like we were family. I've never been the type to express myself openly to others so I would keep things that were on my mind, to myself. I tried to keep peace and remain respectful no matter how I felt, but one time I did get rude with my grandfather's wife when I visited and my grandfather yelled at me. I didn't like making my grandfather upset; he did so much for my family so the last thing I wanted to ever do was make him upset. Although my grandfather was one of the most important people in my life, I didn't express to him how I felt about his wife. I still visited and stayed with them but I kept my peace and didn't say much, I stayed in the basement a lot when I visited and stayed at their house. She's been "grandma" to my siblings and I since we were younger; she's a good person and I feel a lot more comfortable around her now!

After I turned eighteen I began traveling to Maryland at least twice a year to visit my family. My older brother and I were never really close but we hardly ever fought; of course we got into a few arguments and minor tussles when we were children though. I'd arrange for myself and all four of my younger siblings to go to Maryland to visit our family. Even me being in Greensboro which is an hour from Charlotte, I still saw my younger siblings a lot and I remained close to them. So it felt good being able to go get them from Charlotte and spend time with them. My younger four siblings have different fathers from the one my brother and I share. My sister that's behind me in age (Sheriliah), called our father daddy because he'd been in her life since she was a baby. I think my sister stopped calling my father daddy when she was about eighteen. Most children would probably get jealous when their siblings who had different fathers would call their father daddy, but I never remember having a problem with it. I honestly thought for a while that my father was my sister's father. Going to Maryland was fun and all five of us enjoyed it. I still didn't see my maternal grandmother's side of the family, but I wanted to.

I had a lot of unanswered questions regarding my past that needed to be answered but the person I was, I didn't care to tackle those questions. I saw my father from time to time, but didn't see him as much as I should've. Before we moved to NC I recall seeing and spending a lot of time with my father, it would only make sense anyway sense we all lived in the same city. A lot of girls that have relationships with their fathers are labeled "daddy's girls," and that was me and my father. My father had both of his parents in his life when he was growing up; they were happily married until my grandfather passed away in 1992. So I didn't express to my father how much he missed out of his children's lives when we were younger, I just accepted things as they were. My brother and I really didn't have a relationship with our father when we moved and continued to live in NC, because we hardly saw him. The times we saw our father was when we went to Maryland and the two or three times he traveled from MD to see us. It wasn't until I was in my mid-twenties that I sat down and

Relationships

talked to my father about a lot of things that were heavy on my mind and heart. My father had been going through a lot of financial difficulties so he asked could he come and live with me for some time out of the summer, in my apartment in Greensboro. Everyone that knows me knows I'm a very helpful person and regardless of what people go through that I come in contact with, I try my best to lend a helping hand. So my father came to live with my son and I for about two months out of the summer. At the time I had two cars so he drove one of them. He had gotten a job so he needed transportation to get to and from his job. I'm a strong willed individual and I haven't always been able to express myself but I eventually gained the characteristic in my mid-twenties to be a woman that could express her feelings. I'm not sure why I took so long to open up about some of my feelings and concerns regarding my childhood, but it occurred around the time he was leaving from staying with me. I admit I caught attitudes here and there with my father during his stay and during some of our interactions, and my father didn't like it which is understandable. One particular incident involved my father traveling from Greensboro to Charlotte to go see my mother. I felt as if he was making those efforts to go and see my mother but he couldn't make those efforts to go see my brother and I like that when we were younger. My father had every right to go and see his ex-wife and I was aware of that, but I was just so upset about a lot of things that I never expressed to him. Another factor was that my younger three siblings were still in high school and living at home with my mother. So all I could think about was the fact that another man would come into their lives and tell them what to do and how to do it, similar to the things that happened when I was younger when certain men came into our home. One other important issue that still pops in my head to this day is when I was younger and my father married this one lady. She didn't seem too fond of my brother and I but we respected her because she was my father's wife. When her and my father got married my brother and I weren't even involved in the wedding whatsoever, but her son and grandson were both in the wedding. It seemed like a smack in the face because we are family and we traveled from North Carolina to Maryland for the special occasion, but I never talked to my father about that even though it hurt. Growing up in Charlotte I witnessed a lot of verbal, mental, emotional, and even physical abuse from men towards women and a lot of this occurred in my home. My mother was very stern and strict, especially towards me who is her oldest daughter. I never understood why I had so many responsibilities especially always having to care for my three youngest siblings, but I had to do it. One thing I didn't want was for my father to treat my two siblings back home, the way their father treated my mother and all of us when we were younger and that wasn't good treatment. My two younger sibling's father lived with us for a long time and he wasn't a terrible guy but he did things that my sister (Sheriliah), older brother (Anthone), and I, didn't like at all. He drank a

Relationships

lot of alcohol and could often be very mean to his own two children. It's one thing for children to respect their parents but to fear your parents isn't a good thing, and I saw that in my younger three siblings towards this particular man. I really didn't fear him but I didn't like a lot of things he did and how he treated my mother a lot of times. One person I feared was my mother, so I was too scared to tell her how I felt about their relationship. I think that's a big reason as to why I never really bothered watching my younger siblings, because I hated to see them so scared of him. My sister (Netra) has always been emotional and with that being said she'd cry over the smallest things; both of us share that same emotion. I was and still am very emotional, a lot of times just having my younger siblings with me would make me feel at ease. Having them with me let me know that they would be safe and out of harm's way. My father going to visit my mother for the weekend just put a lot of bad memories in my head from when I was younger. One night I recall my mother and this particular man get into a physical altercation and my older brother intervened. My brother intervened to try to help my mother and that man put his hands on my brother. For some reason probably dealing with safety due to us living in the projects, we kept an aluminum bat behind our front door. Anyway, my brother tried using the bat on him to defend our mother but her boyfriend at the time and younger sibling's father, hit my brother. Our apartment was two stories and I was upstairs in my room listening to the entire incident, but I refused to go downstairs and intervene because I hated

Chenelle M. Wiles

conflicts with a passion, and still do. That was just one of the numerous altercations and I wondered when would the fighting ever stop. My mother was strong in a lot of areas but I saw her weakness and it was in men. She put up with too much from men that she shouldn't have, I always thought she should've set a better example for her four daughters. My father told me during our long talk before he went back to Maryland, that he didn't realize how much I went through and he apologized for not being there like he should've for my brother and I. I knew that he should've been more of a dedicated father to his two children, but at that moment I set aside my personal issues with my father and I accepted his apology. That was the first time I ever recall my father apologizing for not being there when he should've been as a father, so that was a humbling experience and it felt sincere. He didn't realize the impact that he could've had on his children's lives because he wasn't around, regardless of the fact that my mother moved us to another state. My mother had to better her and her children's lives no matter what anybody else thought. It seemed like my mother was doing well for herself because soon she dated a guy that me and all of my other siblings liked. This particular man didn't get into altercations with my mother, we often heard him tell her that he wasn't going to argue with her. That was a change for us because we heard a lot of arguing and other negativity with her last boyfriend that lived with us. This man had a son of his own and we all got along with him, he was younger than all of us and about seven months younger than my younger

Relationships

brother. Only thing that didn't sit right about this man was that he had a drug addiction problem. He and my mother stayed together for a few years and when I was a senior in high school, I hardly saw him anymore. Even though my mother wasn't dating or dealing with my younger two sibling's father any longer because of the craziness that went on between them two, we remained close to a lot of his family. A lot of his family lived in the same neighborhood that we lived in. Even though they were only blood related to my younger two siblings, they considered us family and we considered them family.

Bonding with family was always fun and full of surprises, some good and some bad. I can recall a few family reunions on my maternal grandfather's side of the family, a lot of family attended the reunions from all over the east coast of the country. As a teenager my mother, my siblings, and I didn't make it to a few of the earlier reunions but the few we did make it to, things didn't go so well at times. Howard Family Reunions only occurred every other year; consisted of three day events. Family members enjoyed one another and got to know each other, but everyone didn't keep in touch so a lot of us only saw distant family members once every two years for a few days. My grandfather would be recognized at all of the family reunions because of his longevity of family dedication, strong will, and unconditional love to everyone. He's the oldest of my great grandmother's thirteen children and only surviving male. One of his sisters which is my great aunt (Aunt Bett) contributed a lot and resides in New York. She traveled from New York to North Carolina and all other destinations, to participate in the many family events we had. My grandfather and aunt organized a lot of great events and for that reason alone they kept us together as a family. After a while when I was about twenty or so, my mother and older brother stopped attending the family reunions. I continued to attend and participate in the reunions and I took all of my younger siblings with me. The Howard family had a lot of opportunities to build and have relationships with one another, due to the various family events we had to spend time with each other.

    I always wanted to get back in touch with my maternal grandmother's side of the family, but it didn't happen until I was in my mid-twenties. I had gotten in touch with one of my favorite cousins whom is eight years older than me (Troy), and the same one that was raised by my grandmother until she passed. My mother and I were never close but I began to ask her questions regarding our family when I was in my early twenties. Her mother had three children but I only knew one of my aunts, which is my mother's oldest sister. I would often see another aunt when I was younger before we moved to NC, but didn't know until I got older that she was my grandmother's second daughter. This particular aunt was put up for adoption when she was born due to my grandmother being legally married to my mother's oldest sister's father. To this day I'm still confused about the story but I know my

Relationships

mother has two older sisters. My older brother, sister, and I would usually see and spend time with my mother's oldest sister in Maryland and we always had fun. I can recall us going to her house and spending time with her and her boyfriend at the time, he was full of fun. He's deceased now but I just thank God for the memories I have of him. Just like my mother up and left Maryland, my aunt got missing for a while. There are still a lot of questions that need to be answered about how and why a lot of people in the Washington (maternal grandmother) family lost contact. I heard things about my grandmother's house and who it would go to, after she passed. Some of the family got into confrontations dealing with the will and her house I believe, and I heard so many stories but to this day I still don't know the total truth. I guess some information is better when it's left alone, and some information I just didn't ask about. My aunt had left and went somewhere and most of the family didn't talk to her for a few years, but she showed up at my grandfather's house some years later. I remember my mother calling me to tell me that my aunt was going to live with her in Charlotte, and my aunt was coming from my grandfather's house in Camp Springs Maryland. From that day in January of 2008, she stayed close to our family. My aunt helps keep our immediate family together, she always emails and text messages everyone, and cooks good food when we have family get togethers. My aunt wasn't in touch with our family for a few years and it happened a few times, for a period of time. I know when my grandmother was alive she kept the family intact so after she passed it was very difficult for my mother and aunt. My mother and aunt talked a few times out of the years but nobody else talked to my aunt and didn't see her as well. I was close to her when I was a young child but as I got older I wasn't close to her at all. My sister (Sheriliah) and my aunt, became very close. They talked to each other a lot on the phone as well as seeing one another on a regular basis. As an adult besides communicating with my grandfather on the phone and seeing him whenever we traveled, I didn't have a single family member that I was close to. I always talked to my younger siblings and saw them but being older than them, I couldn't talk to them about the things I had on my mind. I was often hurting inside but them being so young, they wouldn't or couldn't relate or be able to give me the feedback I needed to use in life. I often spent a little time with my paternal grandparents as a young child, but my brother and I didn't connect with them a lot. My father's parents lived in Queens New York and we stayed with them a little while in the summer when we were young children, but other than that we didn't spend much time with them. My grandparents eventually moved to Maryland and we saw them a little more (my grandfather passed away in 1992). I enjoyed seeing my paternal grandfather more than my paternal grandmother; it always seemed as if she treated my brother better than she treated me. I didn't have a relationship with her; I loved her but didn't connect with her at all. She passed away in July of 2010. My paternal family is huge and a lot of family members adopted children. My

Relationships

father was adopted by my grandparents at birth. My grandmother's sister adopted children and a few other family members took children in as well. Both my maternal and paternal families had strong relationships with their family at one point in time.

When I moved to Greensboro I remained close to my four younger siblings by talking to them on the phone a lot, visited them at school to eat lunch with them and chaperone field trips, and I'd even take them to Greensboro with me to stay on weekends, holidays, and summer vacations. I was still doing so much for others but wasn't taking time out to make sure I was alright. My younger siblings couldn't take care of themselves and even though my mother was their care taker and sole provider, a lot was going on and I felt as though I needed to continuously help out. The relationship between me and my younger siblings was special; I think they knew they could count on me to be there for them whenever they needed help. I think I started parenthood at the early age of ten when my sister was born and just adapted to all of the responsibilities I had, and I took it into my adulthood when they were a little older as preteens and teenagers. Somehow I had to start having a better relationship with myself, but I didn't know how.

My sister (Sheriliah, behind me in age) had her son when she was a teenager, so I looked out for all of my younger siblings a little more than I looked out for her at that time because his father was in his life. I still did a lot of things for her as well as keeping her son when I went back to Charlotte to spend time with my younger siblings. My mother moved around with us all the time from the time we were in Maryland and when we moved to Charlotte. At one point in time after I left Charlotte for college, my mother and siblings moved to South Carolina. I traveled about three hours every other weekend to see my siblings. My older brother lived with my mother and siblings after he graduated high school until he went into the service as a Marine, in his early twenties. I still didn't branch off from doing so much for my younger siblings yet, too much was going on back home. My mother was going through a lot of financial hardships just like we did when we moved to Charlotte NC, so I felt the need to step up and help so that my family wouldn't go without. I often brought food, took my younger siblings out to eat and to parks to have a good time, and brought them clothes and shoes as well. What was so hard about their fathers stepping up to take responsibility for their children? I couldn't answer that question because my father slacked off of his duties and responsibility as a parent too. At one point in time my two younger sibling's father came back into the picture and lived with my mother and siblings for some time even when they moved to South Carolina, I just couldn't understand it.

    In life certain people come in other people's lives to help and others come in to hurt. The special lady that taught me when I was in the sixth grade took time out to let me know I needed to worry more about myself. I spent a lot of time with

Relationships

her and her family when I was in high school. I went back to find her after I went to the seventh grade which was the start of my junior high school years. Thankfully she was still working at the elementary school she taught me at the year before. I couldn't spend much time with her when I was younger during junior high, due to me doing a lot of things at home dealing with keeping my younger three siblings on a consistent basis. When I did start to hang outside I mainly hung around younger people, I guess it was in my nature due to me having my younger siblings so much. When I went outside I usually had my siblings with me. Towards the end of my tenth grade and entering my eleventh grade of high school, I started to spend more time with Miss Turner who had then become my God sister. She took me to get my hair professionally done in a salon when I was fifteen years old. As I look back on the experience it's funny and we laughed about how my toes were curling and eyes were watering because the relaxer burned my head, but indeed that was the result of what happened from me not realizing that all of my scratching would end up hurting me. From that point in my life, I continued to get my hair done for many years to come. As I continued to spend more time with my God sister, I hardly spent any time at all in the neighborhood I lived in. She was a big sister to me and she encouraged me to do whatever it took to make something positive out of my life. She took me on a visit to her alma mater, N.C. A&T S.U.; I later attended that same college. I didn't often experience many positive things outside of my neighborhood; I'm grateful to

Chenelle M. Wiles

my God sister for opening a positive door for me. I still had responsibilities at home with my siblings but they were cut down a little. My mother started to give me some freedom and I was so grateful for that! I never had an older sister so from that point on I had an older sister which was my God sister, it was so wonderful! She helped me get prepared for my junior prom; I went with a senior and it was one of the best times I had at that particular high school. I had two best friends that I'd been close to since the seventh grade and one of them had a baby when we were seniors in high school, and I was the Godmother. As time went on I began to do more positive things and I had a job as well. I started to not only enjoy being around my God sister but I was introduced to her family. I was so shocked to see how they treated each other, it wasn't like anything I saw at home. They told each other "I love you," gave each other hugs, and spent time with each other under the same roof without cursing or talking down to one another. I heard a lot of that growing up and most children that are brought up a certain way tend to think that that's the way things are supposed to be. My God sister has a sister that's a few years younger than her but she's a few years older than me. Around the time when I was entering my junior year of high school, she was graduating college. I attended her college graduation at the wonderful N.C. A&T S.U. and it was the first time I've ever been to the school I was planning on attending. I was around a lot of their family which I didn't know, and I remember that day so well. It was

Relationships

so lovely being around a big family and having a good time! I was around a lot of older couples that didn't argue, curse each other out, or physically abuse one another. Time went on and they said things to me like "I love you," and I never heard too much of that in my house or in my family. The relationship that I had and still have with them is amazing. If it wasn't for my God sister stepping in to help me, I don't know how I would've made things happen for myself. Not only did my God sister and I become close but I became close with her sister as well, and both of them consider me as their younger sister. All three of us have and still spend a lot of time together; I was in one of their (Tasha) weddings! I enjoy having two older sisters that I can still go to for advice and help, at any time or day. My oldest God sister which is the one who taught me in elementary, got married when I was in high school but my mother wouldn't allow me to go to her wedding so it was wonderful to be a part of my other God sister's wedding. I didn't attend my oldest God sister's wedding but I was present when she gave birth to her daughter which is my niece and that was a very special day for me. Only person that was allowed in the operating room was her husband due to her having a C-section birth, but right afterwards I was one of the first to see my niece along with her family when she was born. My God sister (Tasha) later had a young girl come into her life, after she taught her in one of her middle school classes. They became close and the relationship they share is very similar to the relationship that Shawn and I shared when I was younger. Their relationship is like mother and daughter, and mine and Shawn's are like a big sister and little sister relationship. Shawn and I are eleven years apart and my other God sister Tasha and the young girl she taught (who is now a God daughter to her) are twenty something years apart in age; Tasha has a daughter as well. The young girl and I both share the same birthday and we were taught by our God sister/Godmother in the same year, which was sixth grade. It's a true blessing how relationships form and how all four of us got to know each other.

Even though I didn't have a relationship with many of my family members, I experienced a lot about family bonding and love from spending time with my new God family. I've always had a Godmother, which is the lady who my mother named to be my Godmother (Leslie) when I was born. Out of me and my five siblings, I'm the only one who has always had a good relationship with and who has stayed in contact with my God parent since the beginning at birth. I spent a lot of time with her when I was younger before I moved to NC, and always talked to her on the phone. We spent time together in Maryland on occasions and a lot of other times when I went back to MD to visit. My Godmother is very spiritual and talks to me about God.

As far as opposite sex relationships go, I've experienced a lot of good ones and of course some not so good ones. I can recall my first boyfriend when I was about eleven and of course children always go through crushes so I enjoyed being

Relationships

his girlfriend and I think he enjoyed being my boyfriend (laughing to myself). We both lived close to each other, I lived in the projects on the west side of town and he lived in some apartments that weren't considered part of the projects, in a neighborhood right beside mine. As I got older having a boyfriend wasn't important to me, and besides I didn't really do too much aside from babysitting my siblings and hanging out with other neighborhood children from time to time. I was in a serious relationship when I was in the eleventh grade in high school, but it didn't last too long. He and one of his good friends would always come to my neighborhood because his friend dated one of my female associates. From that point on I went out with guys every once in a while; being a little older I was allowed to go out from time to time but things were still a little strict for me. I guess it was good that my mother was so strict towards me because she didn't want me to make some wrong decisions and mess my life up. Then on the other hand I tend to think why rules always were too strict for me but easy going for my other siblings. I don't regret having things how they were when I was younger because everything I went through made me the strong, independent, intelligent, and caring woman I am today. I dated a few more guys when I moved to Greensboro for college, but I never stayed in relationships too long. If a guy ever did or said anything that made me think they weren't who I needed to be with, I would often fade back from them and the relationship. I hardly took any guys around my family, it wasn't chosen like that it was just the fact that I was in

Chenelle M. Wiles

Greensboro which was an hour from my hometown of Charlotte so we spent a lot of time in Greensboro. I give credit to all of the guys I dated and went out on dates with in college; I was never physically disrespected. I witnessed a lot of physical altercations in relationships growing up and I always promised myself I wouldn't put up with that because I saw too much of it growing up. So to this very day I not only say it but I prove that with my actions. When I continued to get older I had longer relationships with the guys I dated and a few went around some of my family. When my son came into my life I was very careful who I dated and more so, who I decided to have in our home. My son got along with the few guys I dated and he even spent time with them, and to this day he still can hang out with a few of my close guy friends. I have a couple of important guys that are in my life now; I've known one in particular since we were teenagers and I never gave him the time of day(as he always tell me) when we were younger, but we got in touch with one another years later as we were adults. I enjoy doing different things with the different male friends that are in my life! I don't think single people should put a title on certain relationships. I'm very close to a few that I can really connect with because of the common interests we share. I know how women should be treated and I know more importantly how I want to be treated, and it's with respect and genuine love. I still keep in touch with guys I've been friends with for about ten years, it's good having friend relationships with males. Now at this stage I'm in with my life, I'm happy and blessed. I don't and

Relationships

never was at a stage where I thought I needed a man to validate me. It doesn't matter how old I am, I'm going to make myself happy by doing the things I love. I date off and on and I'm currently close to one guy friend in particular, so wherever we go in life together it's what God wants. I'm happy and I'll be pleased as long as it's meant for me.

I haven't always had a lot of friends, then again the word friend means a lot to me. Growing up I had two best friends that remained best friends from our seventh grade in junior high school all the way up to my junior year in high school. When I became a senior in high school I drifted off and went to a different high school than everyone else in my neighborhood as I mentioned earlier. So, I wasn't hanging around them much but I continued to acknowledge them as my best friends because they were. I left for Greensboro and still kept in touch with them for a few years, but I couldn't get in touch with them after that. As years went by we got in touch with one another and even though we didn't have the close bond we did when we were younger, we still remain friends. I have friends and value friendship in the friends I have. I met a lot of wonderful people my senior year of high school; a lot of us went to the same college and we still keep in touch. I'm so grateful for the relationships I have with so many people and friends, even the many people I met when I moved to Greensboro, it's amazing to see the progress I've made in my life and I owe it to so many people! Of course we all go through relationships that aren't good in life whether they're with family, boyfriends and girlfriends, spouses, or whatever the case may be. We just have to learn from the damaged relationships and either improve them or move on. Some relationships just can't be repaired; I've learned that from a lot of relationships I've seen with people I know. I've hurt people and have been hurt so I know very well about the ups and downs of friends and going through bad situations.

Relationships can either make or break us and depending on what obstacles take place, things can be resolved. More than any relationship I've ever encountered, I'm grateful for the relationship I have with God; everything is possible because of Him! Without Him there is no me and I wouldn't have been able to share my life story with the world without Him!!!!!

4. New Life (D.A.W.)

January 20, 2006 was the day that I legally adopted my son! Nine months prior I welcomed him into my home, I was twenty-four and he had just turned twelve. I previously worked with my son in the year of 2004 when I worked for a Group Home that he was placed in. When I worked with him I got to know a lot about him and what was going on in his life. He was the youngest of four children at the time; he had one older brother and two older sisters. Him, his brother, and his sisters were born in Durham North Carolina which was forty-five minutes away from where I was living which was Greensboro NC. My son was the only child of him and his siblings that were living in Greensboro, his other three siblings were in other placements at that current time. He had been in the custody of the State's Department of Social Services since he was two. He had been placed in a few homes, then was adopted by a couple in Greensboro who had no other children. Things didn't work out so he was placed in the group home where I was employed.

When I first met my son he was eleven years old and was in the fourth grade at a close by elementary school. He's very intelligent and math was his favorite subject. He loves football; his favorite NFL team was and still remains the Dallas Cowboys. He loves listening to music, enjoys playing chess, and has so many other interests! He had his ups and downs in the group home like the other children in the facility, but he was very unique and special. He was rather tall for his age as well, with big feet. He enjoyed laughing a lot

Chenelle M. Wiles

and making other people laugh and I noticed that he was very emotional. I can recall a time in which I and a few of my coworkers took the children on a trip somewhere and one song came on the radio while we were riding in the vehicle. Well that must've meant something to him because out of nowhere he began to cry and couldn't stop. It was a motivational and spiritual song by R.Kelly titled "I Wish." I guess the words and meaning of the song got him thinking about a lot of things that had been going on in his life. He got into trouble every once in a while due to him not thinking before he acted. He didn't like talking about his biological family or some of the previous families he resided with, but he talked about one placement he was with when he lived in Durham. He liked that particular placement but had behavioral issues so he had to relocate to a different placement that could better help him with his issues. Due to him moving around frequently he had previously repeated one of his elementary grades, so he was a year behind.

After a year and some of being in the group home, things were coming along for him. His social worker and other team members involved with him had found a potential family for him to live with. He had visited his brother which is three years older than him. His brother was in a foster home which was two hours away from Greensboro and they hadn't seen one another in a few years. Both of them were in a residence together when they were younger but couldn't stay

D.A.W

together long due to both of them presenting extreme behavioral issues. So midway through the summer of 2004 my son successfully moved on from the Group Home where I was employed, and he went to a foster home in Reidsville NC which is a small city very close to Greensboro. This family considered of a married couple with no other children in the home. We held a celebration at the home for him before his departure and he left with the new family he was then set to be with.

As days and months went by, he often called us back at the group home to say hello and let us know how he was doing. He had also gotten on a local recreational football team in that area. He started the last year of his elementary years, which was fifth grade. After a while we hardly heard from him anymore which we expected to be a good thing because usually that meant the child was adjusting well and moving on with their life. His social worker at the time kept in contact with us after a short time because she had another child that she was a social worker for, which was placed in our facility. One of my good friends at that time who was also working at the group home and I, started asking his social worker how he was doing. She would often let us know that he was experiencing some difficulties in school due to his behavior. All of these changes had occurred but we didn't know because we didn't hear from him for a period of time. Some children after they left called back and let the group home

Chenelle M. Wiles

staff know how they were doing, and some didn't. Things began to spiral out of control and he was eventually taken out of that home, and placed in a therapeutic foster home back in Greensboro, until placement could be found for him. In between that time my good friend who was also the weekend Supervisor at the group home and I, went to see him when he was in the hospital. A lot of things that weren't so good took place in that particular foster home that he went to when he left the group home; a lot stemmed from his extreme behavioral issues and a lot stemmed from the way in which his foster parents handled him. After we saw him in the hospital my friend and I talked about some possibilities of how we could help him. He stayed in the hospital for a few days, and that visit was from him getting really sick and his temperature shot up too high. After that he caught an infection that ended up spreading to his hip so it caused him the inability to walk for a few days. While he was in the hospital my friend and I talked a lot about him, she soon encouraged me to think about taking him into my home and being his foster mother.

At that time I was twenty-four, I had a two bedroom apartment to myself, and was still working at the group home. My friend and coworker at the time had a set of twin girls that were about eight years old at the time, and living in a two bedroom apartment as well. She was the weekend supervisor and was only working on the weekends, so she could be with her daughters during the week. So making a

D.A.W

long story short, she suggested that I take him in my home and life. I thought about it for a little while but I had a lot to think about. There was still about two months left in the school year so I didn't know how I would properly care for him. He had to go to school, but I was working Mondays thru Fridays from 3:00-11:00 p.m. My friend was working on weekends so she suggested that she'd keep him during the week after school until the following mornings. Indeed, we had a plan to help better the life for D.A.W. These plans came about during February and March of 2005. Plans seemed to be falling into place; I just had to get thoroughly assessed by Social Services and my apartment had to get inspected, to ensure safety for D.A.W. He was excited about the transition approaching but I think I was more excited than he was! One thing that was certain was that I had a wonderful friend who encouraged me to take the step in helping D.A.W, and he also had a dedicated and supportive Social Worker!

After the paperwork went through he finally came to my home in April of 2005. The first weekend he was with me I took him to the local carnival that was in town. We rode a few rides and ate some snacks; I remember it like it was yesterday. For that next week I had to transport him to and from school, which was the same school he was attending in Reidsville when he resided in the last foster home. We traveled about thirty minutes to and from his school for that week; this was done so he could finish his End of Grade testing. After he completed his testing he went back to the elementary school that he attended when he was living in the group home. He loved it because most of his friends, the same principal, and teachers from the previous year were still there. For the next two months my son stayed at my friend and former coworker's house after school, and spent the night during the school week. I picked him up in the mornings to take him to school. On weekends we did a lot of things, sometimes we stayed at home and sometimes we went to Charlotte to see family. Other times we simply just enjoyed ourselves hanging out in Greensboro doing various other things in the surrounding areas. Although he had behavioral issues at the elementary school in Reidsville, he did well at the elementary school that he returned to when he came to live with me in Greensboro.

Seems like a new life was taking place for D.A.W! I wasn't sure how things would unfold but I was happy and he seemed to be happy as well. He was receiving individual therapy to help him cope with the many changes he had experienced in his life. He was tested for a hand tremor he had and he had that issue for quite some years, but doctors and specialists couldn't find out what it was stemming from. I believe it came from him being medicated for so many years. I've never been a fan of medication and I took steps to get him off of his medications. I feel as though any individual will adapt to something if it's been connected to them for a long time and that was what I felt about the medications he was prescribed to for his ADHD. My son also had a thumb sucking habit and

D.A.W

had that habit since he was very young. He continued that habit for a long time afterwards until he had to get braces, and I have yet to see the habit spark up again. He entered his first year of middle school which was the sixth grade, in the fall of 2005. He started to struggle behavioral wise constantly in school. He didn't like to be told what to do by any authority in the school setting, and the least little thing he was told to do he exploded. He has always been intelligent and often enjoyed helping his teachers. D.A.W. seemed to love keeping his hands moving, it was probably due to the hand tremor he had. He was suspended from school a lot for his disrespectful and disruptive behaviors. At home I didn't have many problems out of him but it was very stressful trying to help him overcome his unacceptable behavior that he presented with all other authority figures, especially in school. School continued to be difficult for him and he continued to act out in the seventh grade. His behaviors were beyond out of control and I implemented punishments at home but it only seemed that he had adapted to being punished so much, that he didn't care what the outcome of his behaviors were. Although he was getting therapy every week and had been for a few years, something seemed to be missing. He was reluctant to discuss anything relating with his biological family, but the only family members he would ever talk about seemed to be his three older siblings particularly his older brother. I had a few guy friends that often talked to him and spent time with him. I knew I was doing a lot to help D.A.W., I just wanted him to take some steps to help himself but he either didn't know how or wasn't willing to do so.

During the middle of my son's seventh grade year I took it upon myself to take him out of that middle school setting and put him into a smaller and more structured setting school. This school had two teachers and about four more adults that helped with the students. There were about fifteen students total and they were split into two classes. I really enjoyed the teachers as I did in the previous school; they generally cared for D.A.W. so much and were always there to help him. More than anything, they put up with a lot from him that they didn't need to. Things didn't seem to work out at this school either so I had to get some other things in place. Before he left his middle school he threatened one of his teachers so he was placed on probation in the juvenile court system. He was on probation for some time and I recommended that he be punished by the court system. We went to court and the judge asked for my opinion; I let her know that he needed to be held responsible for his negative actions so he was ordered to spend a weekend in the local juvenile detention center which is a jail for children.

Shortly after his stay in the detention center, I had arranged for something else that was more strict and structured to fall into place. Everything that had been planned out to help him wasn't working so I had to see what other options would work for him. Myself and my son's case manager arranged for him to go to a Wilderness Camp. The

D.A.W

process for the Wilderness Camp was hectic at first because he didn't have enough points in the legal system for them to make a referral to go to the camp. I felt as if the judicial system wanted him to get into more trouble before he could be looked at for a program such as a Wilderness Camp. I turned to his social worker for some help, that's when the case manager came in the picture. He had two case managers, one was a female and the other was a male. The process was finally underway and in July of 2007 he went to Wilderness Camp; it was about an hour and fifteen minutes away from Greensboro. He and I had talked a few times before the process started and he was on board with it. He often used two favorite phrases to describe his feelings and they were "I don't care" and "It doesn't matter to me." Whenever he did something wrong or consequences came into play, he would usually use those phrases.

 Wilderness Camp for D.A.W. was another intervention to help him better manage his behaviors and cope with various situations. His first two months there, he stayed at camp night and day. He had school, participated in group exercises, and slept in a large tent with tarp on the top; in which some of the campers helped build. Swimming and craft activities were held as well. This was an all-male camp for troubled young males. D.A.W. ended up staying at the camp for thirteen months. He experienced a lot of struggles, mainly dealing with respect which was his downfall. We wrote each other letters a few times out of the months and he was able to call and talk to me one day out of every week for about ten to fifteen minutes. He often came home at least twice a month for a few days on the weekends to implement life skills he learned at camp, and to basically be with family. I got in touch with his home school which was the middle school he previously attended before going into the smaller setting school, then Wilderness Camp. I talked to a few of his teachers and the principal to see if he could attend school on those Fridays that he was home, which were generally two Fridays out of the month. No matter how much D.A.W. disrespected them and disrupted their school, they knew he had great potential and they wanted to continue helping him succeed. So he went to school twice a month on Fridays to help out one of his former teachers, and that went well. Sometimes he didn't come home due to his behavior, and the camp didn't approve of home visits if campers were exhibiting major behavioral issues.

    D.A.W. stayed at the camp until August of 2008 when he graduated and came home, after thirteen long months. He had been there a long time and was still doing inappropriate things mainly being disrespectful up until the very day he left. No matter what help or intervention is thrown at any individual that struggles with something, it's up to them to decide if they want to take advantage of the help that's offered and change. At that moment that's what I had to do; I didn't look into anymore programs for my son from that point on. Indeed he needed to live a productive life and at fifteen I

D.A.W

knew he was capable of making better decisions. About three weeks prior to him graduating from Wilderness Camp, I began doing some searching. From the time I got D.A.W. in my home, I always let him know that it was his decision if he wanted to see and have a relationship with his biological family. He had always told me in return that he didn't want to get in touch with anyone but his older brother and two older sisters. He remembered his biological mother, father, and older siblings, but he didn't remember anyone else from his biological family. He lived with his father for a short period of time when he was younger but was moved to another placement shortly after for some reason.

Three weeks prior to him graduating from Wilderness Camp, I searched on the internet for his biological mother. It didn't take long and it wasn't too difficult for me to locate her. I got a telephone number for her and soon called her. I remember one of the first things I did when we talked on the phone that first time was ask her if I contacted the right person after I stated her name. She indeed let me know that she was that person. I let her know that I was D.A.W.'s mother and that I was trying to get in touch with her because he wanted to get in touch with his siblings. We talked for a while and I let her know that he had some difficulties so he was away at a camp to help him get things in order with his behavior, and he would be leaving camp soon to come home. I explained to her that I'd talk to him the upcoming weekend to let him know I located her so he could get in contact with his siblings. I didn't give her any information as to how she could get in contact with him, for the simple reason being that I wanted to talk to him first to see how he felt about the information. In the meantime she let his siblings know that she knew D.A.W. was doing alright and that they might be seeing him sometime. She had three children younger than D.A.W. that he never met, so she had seven children in all.

When my son came home for his last home visit before he was scheduled to graduate from Wilderness Camp, we had a long talk in the car. I let him know that I located his biological mother (I called her by her name when I talked to him due to him doing it because he called me mom). I never kept any information from him and I felt no need to do so. On his first day of middle school he decided on his own to use my last name when his teachers and other school faculty addressed him, on all of his assignments, and in general. All of his teachers approved for him to do that and let me know that it was ultimately his decision, so they honored it. He was adopted once before when he was younger and that occurred when he first moved to Greensboro, then again when it was by me in January of 2006. So with that being said he chose to address me as mom and to everyone he talked to concerning me, as mom. D.A.W. let me know that he did want to talk to and see his siblings. When he went back to camp for the last few weeks before graduating, I contacted his biological mother on my way home. I talked to her letting her know, that he wanted to see and talk to his siblings. She seemed

D.A.W

very excited and she immediately let her children know the good news.

In August when D.A.W. graduated from Wilderness Camp, he told me that he changed his mind and didn't want to go with his original plan to visit his siblings. I let him know whatever decision he made it was his decision, and I had no other choice but to respect that. I wasn't sure as to why he decided not to go through with the plans to see his siblings which in fact were the people he often talked about, but it was obviously something he thought long and hard about. So he chose not to go visit them and he hadn't seen them in years, but I had to let them know. Not long after our conversation (probably a few days afterwards), I called his biological mother and let her know he changed his mind. I hadn't communicated with her in about two weeks or so, since our conversation regarding D.A.W.'s original decision to see his siblings. When we talked she let me know that my son's older brother had gotten incarcerated; this was some heart breaking news that I had to deliver to D.A.W. The conversation between him and I was very emotional on his part and I comforted him like a parent is supposed to.

Even though he decided not see his siblings at that time, he communicated with both of his older sisters over the telephone. Him and his sisters kept in touch with one another by phone for quite a while; one of his sisters called him on a regular basis to talk to him. Then in December of that same year, his oldest sister had a baby so I took him to Durham to visit them in the hospital. That was the first time he saw his sister since he was younger, so they certainly enjoyed the time they had with each other. His biological mother was going to come to the hospital to see D.A.W. but didn't make it, so we headed back to Greensboro that night (we were not sure as to why she didn't get to make it to the hospital). A few months later on one afternoon before going to one of his therapy appointments, he asked me to help him find what correctional facility his brother was located at so he could write him. On one of the many days when he was on punishment due to his inappropriate and disrespectful school behavior, he wrote his brother a letter. He's a very thoughtful and intelligent young man and when he puts his mind to it, he does awesome things. Him and his brother wrote one another for a short time, and I was happy to see them communicating. He didn't communicate with his sisters much anymore for a while and he only spoke to his biological mother a few times. He had their contact information and they had his so the lines of communication were available, everybody just slacked off and didn't contact one another for a while.

    Things continued to spiral out of control for D.A.W. with his constant behavioral issues in school, and at the same time he was able to do well on his school work. He was constantly disrespecting teachers, disrupting class, and also getting

D.A.W

suspended from school. Me being a single parent to a teenage male became very stressful. I continued to implement some punishments with him at home, which stemmed from no phone to no outside, to him not even being able to have snacks; food and snacks are things that he adored just like most young males. He presented issues in school throughout his entire freshman year of high school. The high school he attended was a transition school from the middle school he attended, which was directly beside one another. We had numerous talks and he sometimes told me "I'm going to act right," or "I didn't do anything wrong," to "I don't care" which seemed to be his favorite phrase. He was a regular and normal child at home meaning I had to get on him from time to time about different things, but he wasn't and never presented many major problems at home. His teachers and various other faculty members at his high school always complimented his intelligence and willingness to help teachers a lot, but couldn't understand why he had trouble with his behavior. He was on the high school's football team and is a very talented football player. I often took him off of the practice field and didn't let him play in weekly school football games, because of his behavior and disrespect towards teachers. I knew that he had to learn one way or another that he couldn't treat people any kind of way then expect to do the things he loved and enjoyed; that wasn't going to fly with me. I've always heard people say that "It takes a man to raise a man," that's probably true but I was going to do whatever it took to raise my son to be a respectful young man. I can recall when my son was in middle school; I had a reward system for him set up by keeping a track of his behavior on charts, which enabled him to earn weekly allowance. One time he earned the reward to visit Duke University in Durham NC, which was the school he always talked about attending for college. He, another female mentee which was about four years older than him, and I all went to the college one day for a tour. We ate lunch in the cafeteria and really enjoyed ourselves! He had his ups and downs; meaning he had some good days and he also had some bad days. When he was in the seventh grade I had him get a book signed daily by each of his teachers, letting me know how his behavior had been in each class. As he got older there were no incentives, I continued expressing to him that he needed to do what was expected of him for himself and not for rewards. D.A.W. was also still consistently receiving weekly therapy during all of this time.

 We moved to a different residence in Greensboro so his school district had changed. I took the liberty of going to the local school assignment center to get approval for him to remain at the school he had been attending, because I didn't approve of him going to the school that was assigned to the neighborhood we moved to. It wasn't a personal issue with the school; I mentored a few young people that attended that school. I just felt as though a change that drastic

D.A.W

would further hold him back from improving his behavior and respect. I also knew that this different school had predominantly African American students and the one he'd been attending was mixed with a few different races, so I thought he needed to be around diversity as much as possible. The first reassignment request that I put in, was denied. So I did an appeal and when that happened it took place at the school assignment office, in front of a few school board members. In the meeting I voiced my opinion about the need for my son to succeed and I let them know that I'd rather leave him at his current school at the time due to the drastic change, his constant behavioral issues we were trying to tackle, and the fact that he didn't need to be in a school with all African Americans due to him acting out a lot for attention anyway. I had to keep some stability in his life and continuing to move him to different schools wasn't doing that at all. The board listened to everything I had to say, and the decision was overturned so that meant my son was approved to remain at the school he was currently attending. He was placed on a contract explaining that I had to provide transportation to and from school for him, so he wasn't allowed to ride the school bus due to him no longer being in the school district. He couldn't get into any trouble whatsoever, which was explained to him by me after I attended the appeal. I explained to him that he needed to realize that I took off work and went through drastic measures to keep him in that particular school to help him

Chenelle M. Wiles

succeed. Of course he told me he was going to change by being respectful and staying out of trouble.

    Going into his sophomore year of high school D.A.W. still continued to do the same thing he'd been doing in school; disrespecting teachers and being disruptive. His teachers worked with him and sometimes gave him too many chances, by not letting me know when he misbehaved. I wasn't hearing any negative reports from teachers for about two weeks so I assumed he'd been doing well, I was obviously fooled. One female teacher in particular let me know when I contacted her that he had been talking very rudely to her. When school started that year I set up a system that I'd communicate with his teachers via email, to check on his progress. So I punished him and didn't let him participate in football games as a consequence to him acting out in class. At times he acted like he didn't care about the consequences, but he knew I would continue to be consistent with raising him right. He did little things such as refuse to take his hat off in class when he already knew it was a school rule not to wear hats. Well, write-ups/referrals piled up and eventually the school reassignment office was notified. They sent me a letter and informed me that D.A.W. would have to leave that school due to his behavior and breaking the contract. I was beyond upset with him even before the letter came because I had been letting him know he couldn't continue to treat people so harsh. He loved that school very much;

D.A.W

talked about how much he enjoyed being with all of his friends he'd been growing up with, etc. Around that time I'd been looking for another home, a bigger one to be exact, and in a better neighborhood. Luckily we moved again due to me finding a nice home on the northeast side of Greensboro; so he would be assigned to another school, if not he would've had to go to the school I didn't want him to attend. One thing that was certain, he enjoyed getting negative attention and I always told him that seemed to be the case. He tried apologizing to me for his constant negative behavior and inconvenience to me having to go through drastic measures to help him, but I wasn't moved at all by his apology. Parents have feelings too and the dedicated ones have every right to get frustrated, and frustrated was how I was feeling.

  D.A.W. wasn't receiving therapy any longer at this point in time, which was in the beginning of 2010 and the middle of his sophomore year of high school. His therapist talked to me and let me know he wasn't productive in sessions because he constantly avoided his issues and blamed others for his actions. I agreed with her and let her know that he was sixteen soon to be seventeen, so he had to figure things out on his own. He was done with therapy and no longer took medication due to him needing a break from it. He'd been off of medication for ADHD since he was twelve. My son was on so much medication when he first came into my home, that he was falling asleep at his school bus stop in the mornings. I made the decision right then and there for him to be taken off of medication, so his doctor slowly weaned him off.

    At the end of his sophomore year of high school, D.A.W. went to another high school; this one was for the district in which we moved to at the beginning of April in 2010. So for those few short months he was at that school, we were still at it with his behavior. Letting him know that he needed to build a better reputation for himself at this new school, went in one ear and out the other. He had to wear specific clothing due to this school having a dress code, so I had to go and purchase him clothing for him to wear for the remainder of the school year for him at this current school. He tried one particular stunt in which he did at the previous school, by putting on a hat in class and refusing to take it off. Of course he didn't have a reason for putting up a struggle with his teacher over the rules, he wanted negative attention again. He was on punishment at home after that incident and one day I came home to find this letter on my bed from him:

    I know right from wrong I just don't understand why it's so hard for me to do what's right. I try hard and think a whole lot about what I do or what I'm going to do, but in the end I always seem to do the wrong thing. I'm lost and I don't know what I'm doing with my life. It seems like the longer I don't know what I'm doing with my life. It seems like the longer I don't know the faster I go downhill. I do badly in school but outside of school am good. When I do well in school everything else falls apart. So times I wonder why I'm still here. Why is God letting me live if all I do is put the people

D.A.W

who love me through hell. In the past few weeks I've found myself thinking of others life without me and anyway I look at it, it seems to get better. Life's no fun living by the moment that's nothing but trouble. What's my life with a plan, D.A.W's such a good kid I'm this I'm that. So why can't anything go right? I never thought of life being this shitty, I guess life fits the person living it. Passing time so thought I'd write what's going on in my mind,

D.A.W (4-23-2010)

 I truly believe the summer before D.A.W.'s junior year of high school, he did a lot of thinking about his life. He often thanked me for just being there for him and not giving up on him when other people gave up on him. Certain times he'd come to me and tell me how he talked to people that he witnessed going through things he went through, and how he encouraged them to not make the same mistakes he did. I was so happy and proud of him; I let him know that he just didn't need to tell them that but he needed to be showing proof by his actions. Well thankfully his actions started to show, slowly but surely. The start of his junior year he began to make a few changes by handling situations differently in school. He had a few incidents in school but they weren't occurring as often as they were in the past. I still remained consistent by giving him consequences when he disrespected teachers or acted inappropriate. D.A.W. had to decide on his own that enough was enough and that's when he started to mature. One thing that was evident in school was that he was in fact, still a class clown; he loved making people laugh. In the past he did so many rude and disrespectful things for negative attention, so from this point he gave adults more respect, but was still humorous in school. He is not perfect and nobody is, so even though he still makes mistakes, he has made a great deal of improvements in his life and I am proud of his accomplishments.

We always spent time together but as he got older and more mature, we continued to spend even more time together. A lot of times children and people in general just want people to listen to them. We took trips to Maryland to see family and even went to the beach during Christmas; just the two of us to spend time with one another. He talks to me about a lot of different things; honestly sometimes I can't get him to be quiet. I give him honest advice about what he should do in different situations. I also let him know how he should handle situations, but in the end it's up to him. Talking about things such as sex isn't a problem for me to discuss with my son, if parents don't communicate with their children then they won't know how their children feel about things. Of course children are going to make their own minds up to do what they want, but us as parents still have to set the guidelines and let them know how we feel and what decisions are totally right or wrong. I reflect back on the time not too long after D.A.W. came into my home and life; we went to visit a local Military School. He was very eager to attend the camp that they held during the summer in which he had to wear a military uniform with boots, and go through the lifestyle of a young man in the service. He attended that camp for about five weeks during that summer and he had a wonderful time. Even though it was very structured, he did well with the structure and got a long lasting experience as well.

Time went on during his junior year of high school and I wasn't hearing anything about him disrespecting teachers or being disruptive. Shortly before Christmas of 2010 he began to hear from a lot of his family members on a social internet website. He communicated with them and let them know he didn't remember them. They all remembered him but his memory of them was vague. So they all exchanged phone numbers over the internet and began to verbally communicate. I talked to his paternal grandmother and paternal aunt, and eventually we arranged for him to go and visit them back in Durham NC. So, he stayed in contact with them all for about a month then the time finally arrived; D.A.W. and I traveled from Greensboro to Durham. The ride was about forty-five minutes and the first initial visit was from a Friday evening to a Sunday afternoon. He was so ready to see them and reunite with his cousins, who are mostly all around his age. I took him to his aunt's house and I talked to her in person for the first time, it was a good start so I seemed comfortable and happy that they were all getting a chance to reconnect. After the first weekend he went back a few more times; he loved spending time with his family. I

Chenelle M. Wiles

let him communicate with his family and arrange when he wanted to go spend time with them; he was approaching eighteen so it was his choice to make. When he turned eighteen in March of 2011, he started to do a lot more things and I let him know that many decisions in his life he had to make them on his own. It was totally up to him to initiate with both his family and I to let us know when he was trying to go to Durham. I'm not sure if he was letting his biological family know about arrangements, but he wasn't asking me to take him to Durham much anymore on weekends. I did have a few times in which I wasn't going to make the drive due to me having other things planned as well as me being the only person who was driving him, and gas prices were outrageous. I often asked him did he want to go to Durham, and he let me know he had other things to do on the weekends. I asked him did he communicate that information with his family and he let me know that he did. I'm happy and thankful that he was able to reunite with some of his family. Whenever I talked to any of his family they were very thankful, respectful, and understanding so that said that their character was good. Even as a junior I still stay in touch with his teachers, pop up on him at school, and take care of other responsibilities that parents are supposed to. I did let him know that he was totally responsible for his actions and reactions, and that he needed to always think things through thoroughly before he acts on them. He has not been to jail/prison and I hope it remains that way; we've discussed the fact that I will not support disrespect and crimes that hurt others, and me visiting jails/prisons are really not in my favor.

At this point in time while finishing up the writing process of this book, I am constantly in thought of how far my son has come. D.A.W has made some great accomplishments in his life and I thank God for allowing him to get to the place he is in today! Even though D.A.W has struggled with various things, he is a living testimony of how our youth can make it in life even when they had a rough past. One of his favorite movies when he was younger was the movie Holes; based on a young teenager who was wrongfully convicted of a crime and sent to a detention camp that was located in a desert. The children that were incarcerated at the camp had to dig holes in the desert on a daily basis, and they dug the holes in hot weather most of the time. The main character which was a young teenager, didn't commit the crime that he was charged for but he still did what he had to do to make it out! To make a long story short, this young man helped another young man that was incarcerated at the camp, learn how to read. The two of them became friends and were soon freed from the camp, and reunited with their families! I see similarities in the main character and D.A.W due to their strong will to overcome adversities and still have the heart of gold to help others! My son is still young but he is now a young man instead of a child! He has come a long way in his life and isn't giving up on his positive endeavors!

Chenelle M. Wiles

As D.A.W's junior year in high school is ending, he seems to be on a positive and successful path in life! He has been playing on his school's football teams since he was in the seventh grade; I attend mostly all of his games and I have been his biggest fan! One incident after another continued to happen in school: Even though D.A.W has had many issues in school with respecting authority, he has goals for his future and one main goal is attending college. My son rarely complained of the things he went through in his past; from moving around to different homes, being in the custody of the state, being adopted twice, etc. I know that regardless of how things seemed to other people including myself from time to time, my son had major concerns on his mind all the time in reference with people giving up on him, his life constantly changing, and even worries about his future. My son had a rough past and I wish he would not have gone through so much. As I acknowledge my past struggles in life during my upbringing, I know what doesn't kill us will certainly make us stronger, and I also acknowledge that we can't hold grudges towards those who have done us wrong because we still need to make things right for ourselves. A few months prior to me writing this manuscript, D.A.W turned eighteen. I try to put myself in other people's shoes such as the younger generation, and not be so uptight about the decisions that they make because I once was a child and made many mistakes. So with that said, I've always told my son to be careful of the mistakes he makes because they can hurt him in the long run and damage his career decisions.

D.A.W

In the state in which we live, when you reach the age of sixteen you can legally be tried as an adult if you commit a crime; my son has been to the Juvenile Detention Center but has not been to jail and I am so proud of him for that! A large amount of the young people I used to coach, mentor, or work with are incarcerated and I still communicate with them by writing them letters to the facilities in which they are incarcerated. I want my son to realize that it's alright to make mistakes but it's a problem to make the same mistakes that we made in the past; that means we are not learning from our mistakes or we do not care about the consequences that follow. As my son enters his senior year of High School, I am so proud to be able to witness him on his journey to success! From the time my son came into my life and our home, I devoted so much time to his well-being, education, and so much more that many times I wasn't taking time out to care for myself. If anyone knows anything about being a dedicated parent, then we all know that we must put our children before we put ourselves. I've learned that in many cases involving our youth, when they act out in negative ways, they are seeking attention. Most of the time our young people just want to get a point across and the only way they know how to get their point across is to lash out or be destructive. I am a firm believer of tough love and consequences, but I also had to learn a few times when my son would get into trouble, that I had to listen to what he had to say instead of assuming that he was always at fault; parents learn from their

Chenelle M. Wiles

children just like children learn from their parents. D.A.W has a lot of insight when it comes to analyzing difficult situations and I think much of that has to do with the many challenges and changes he faced during his childhood years. I have been working with youth for many years and one thing that is evident is, they're all different in so many ways so when a challenge arises with a youth, we must evaluate what technique would be appropriate to approach with them. When I am upset I don't like being touched or talked to, I just like being to myself so that I can calm down and think about what is on my mind. In the same regard, D.A.W has been like that for as long as I've known him. I can recall my first week working in the group home in which he resided at the time and another staff member tried to physically remove D.A.W from a difficult situation, which was the wrong thing to do because D.A.W reacted in a physical manner.

   I know that raising a child is difficult but a single parent mother raising a man is one of the hardest full time jobs to attain. D.A.W has made parenting for me, worthwhile. There were so many times that I became stressed out, but regardless of the stress I endured, I will not trade anything in the world for him! The loving bond that I share with my son is unexplainable and for the rest of my life, I will cherish our relationship. A child doesn't have to be born into a family in order for them to be considered family; love is what is important in any relationship. I had a wonderful family take me into their family and to this day, they consider me to be

D.A.W

a part of their family. D.A.W wasn't born into my family but from the day he came into my home, all of my family then became our family! D.A.W has made a connection with some of his family members, specifically his paternal family members. Due to him leaving the city of Durham NC when he was a young child to live elsewhere, his memory faded and he didn't remember most of his family but he has reunited with a lot of his family over the past few months and I am so glad he did.

At this point in time D.A.W is eighteen years old and is still growing into the man he was created to be. I didn't think I would ever say this because it sounded so weird when I heard adults say it when I was a child but: "My baby grew up so fast!" When he came into my life at the age of twelve I didn't know what was in store, only God knew about the plan for me to become his mother and he become my son.

I encourage people to never give up on themselves and put forth every positive effort to make something worthwhile out of life. My son had difficulty with authority and it took him a long time to realize that treating people wrong wouldn't get him anywhere. D.A.W. is far from done with doing wonderful things in his life, but if he puts forth total effort to do what he needs to do to succeed, one step at a time he will conquer his success. I'm sure his life will be successful and he'll be happy as long as he's on the right path and does not hurt people along the way, especially the ones that give their all into helping him.

5. Recovery

If and when things happen that are wrong, how do we recover and make things right? I'm pretty sure this question is often asked numerous times throughout every person's life; I think it depends on the individual and their desire to improve whatever needs to be improved in their life. Some people never recover from the things that hindered them from succeeding in life. Then on the other hand some people do whatever it takes to not go down the same path they were once on, which kept them from moving forward in a positive direction. There are many situations that occur in life and we often can control the situation, then other situations we can't control.

For the past five or six years I often told myself and a few others in my life, that I was going to write a book. As of this current year which is 2011, I put my words into action by starting and completing my book. A lot of things have taken turns for good and bad in my life this year, but things happen in our lives that will either help or harm us. I was diagnosed with Carpal Tunnel Syndrome earlier this year following a car accident I was involved in. Carpal Tunnel didn't stop me from doing something I wanted to do; it most definitely slowed me down due to some pain I often experienced in my wrist from writing and typing so much. That pain was only a minor setback; it's a permanent issue but it will not prevent me from producing the work I promised to myself and others! Even though I was involved in an accident that would cause me to have a disability, I turned it into a success story by

Chenelle M. Wiles

following through with my positive admirations! We may not always be able to recover from difficult situations, but we can make the best out of situations by turning the impossible into possible resolutions.

    Many ordinary people like me have stories to tell about how we overcame adversities and made the best out of tough situations; I continue to make the best out of many situations! We often hear a lot of documentaries about celebrities that have gone through difficult situations growing up, and are now making millions of dollars doing what they love. They're also putting in work by volunteering time and donating money to various organizations. I admire a lot of celebrities for going above and beyond to help others out, now that they're financially able to do so. I'm fully aware that it takes hard work and dedication to make it to successful points in life. So many people that are deceased have paved the way for us to be able to voice our opinions without us having to be incarcerated. They did wonderful things for us to be allowed to sit on public city buses without having to stand up, to be able to drink out of any public water fountain we want, attend various schools regardless of our race, and so much more. There are many people that help our society who aren't celebrities and we don't hear of them as much; like we hear about movie stars, basketball and football players, and so many other famous people. We have numerous people in this society who donate parts of their bodies, to help others that are having difficulties with their bodies, live longer.

Recovery

Then we have other people that are going through such difficult times in life, but decide to take their own lives. When people threaten or actually end up taking their own lives, negotiators are put into those difficult situations. Negotiators step in difficult situations on a consistent basis, to help people realize that their lives are worth living. There are also many coaches that put in much hard work and dedication by helping people learn various skills in life. Professional coaches get paid to coach but there are many unsung heroes such as recreational center coaches and afterschool tutors, who do not get paid to help the people they help; they do it because it's their passion and they wish to show people such as children, that there are positive things to do in life. There are many unsung heroes that go above and beyond to help others get to higher levels in life. LaShawn Summers still remains an influential teacher; I am so proud of her and I often let her know how thankful I am for her! She still teaches sixth graders and does whatever it takes to help young children succeed! Many police officers go out every day and put their lives on the line just like Officers John Burnette and Andy Nobles did in my neighborhood when I was younger. Firefighters, bus drivers, people serving in the military, teachers, and so many other ordinary people are constantly overlooked for their hard work and they too, have recovered from adversities in their lives. They still do what it takes day in and day out, to keep things in good perspectives for themselves and others. I appreciate the hard work and

Chenelle M. Wiles

dedication from any and all people that put in the sweat and tears to make a difference in this world!

I've worked with adolescents that were recovering from substance abuse. Some individuals were born drug addicted so they didn't choose to be in the position they were in. Others choose to get on drugs and that gives them a struggle against themselves. Working in the substance abuse field not only gives me the knowledge about the effect that drugs have on people's lives, it opens my eyes in awareness to the possibilities of drugs taking over and damaging a lot of good relationships. Recovery is a word that's constantly used in the substance abuse field. Recovery is a lifelong process when dealing with substance abuse addictions; it only takes a quick second to go from sobriety to relapse.

At the point in time while I was writing this book, my aunt (mother's sister) had a stroke early one morning. It took me by surprise as well as my family because she's so young and is always doing something to stay active. She sends various family members cards, small gifts, and daily emails to stay connected. Slowly but surely she started recovering and healing; blessings were certainly put all on her. Even though she's still in the recovering stage, things are looking better for her and she's getting the help she needs. I wish my grandmother would've recovered from her sickness and still be alive, but I know that's not possible. I used to think that if she wouldn't have passed away when in the past, that a lot

Recovery

of bad things that happened, wouldn't have (the family not communicating and being distant possibly wouldn't have taken place).

    I still help people but now I put myself first and think more about my well-being, instead of putting myself aside. When we lose out on the love and care for ourselves by taking care of others, we're not getting what we need out of life. It's impossible for us to help others if we can't help ourselves first. Depending on who the individual is and how their process is, recovery could be a very difficult topic. Many people are diagnosed with diseases and they don't recover, others do recover and things start to spark in the right direction for them. Complaining about things that happened to us in our lives won't erase the problems and they won't even help us move on, so we need to acknowledge how we can recover and move on.

    The purpose of me writing this book was to simply let my voice be heard and to make people aware that even though I'm not famous to a lot of people, I can still be publicly heard! We all have dreams and desires in life, but it takes hard work to make it to where we need to be. I don't regret having to struggle in life because I wouldn't be the successful woman I am today, if I wouldn't have fallen and made some mistakes. When I stumbled it might've taken me some time but I got up and kept pushing to stay on the right track. This book is a small token of how life has been for me and no matter how

Chenelle M. Wiles

others view me, I'm proud of the person I am and the things I've done to help others do the right things. I've made mistakes and I will continue to make mistakes, it's all a part of life. There were plenty of times in my life in which I thought I wasn't going to be able to overcome some struggles I endured, but it was the fight in me that kept me going!

I've asked the "why" question so many times throughout my life regarding many situations and obstacles. I asked "Why did my grandmother have to die?" "Why didn't we stay in Maryland instead of move to North Carolina?" "Why do people continue to kill?"- I know the answers to a lot of questions like my grandmother passing away because death is a part of life and it was her time to go. My mother, siblings, and I moved to North Carolina so that my mother could get away and make a new life for all of us .We grew up getting government assistance but I am not ashamed of the help that my family and I received; we all need help at times in our lives. I can remember times in which my mother would send me to one of the corner stores with food stamps to get small items we needed for the house. I'm pretty sure most of the people in my neighborhood when I was a teenager in public housing in Charlotte growing up, received public assistance as well. If it weren't for us moving to NC I probably wouldn't have taken that step of bringing my son into my home and into my life, meeting my second God family, and also being able to expand my skills of helping the youth all throughout Greensboro North Carolina. I've recovered from the inability

Recovery

to acknowledge what love means, to now being the initiator in sharing love to others. People learn different things; sometimes from different people and in different situations. I have two sisters that had children while they were teenagers; of course they struggled but they did what they had to do for their children by providing and staying in high school to complete their education. One of my sisters had her son when she was sixteen; she was at the end of her junior year in high school. She did what she had to do by getting a job, remaining in school, and later on her and her boyfriend (son's father) got a place together. My other sister(Nise) that had twin girls when she was seventeen, decided to move to Greensboro with me the second half of her senior year. The job I was working at, I worked closely with some teachers due to our program having a school. One of the teachers worked at a night school specifically designed for teenagers who needed to complete their high school education. My sister soon attended this school (she couldn't attend her graduation because she went to the hospital three days before the graduation day); she completed her high school education! I recall both of us going to the mall to pick out an outfit for her graduation. So we were heading home and that's when she started to experience pain. We went to the hospital and that's when she was admitted. She was unable to participate in her high school graduation which was on June 5, 2008 and her twin daughters were born on that following day which was June 6, 2008. They all remained in the hospital for a while; the twins were in the Intensive Care Unit due to them being born premature and having some breathing difficulties. Now the twins are three and so full of joy! That entire recovery process was and still is a true blessing.

Starting from somewhere and making the very best out of situations is how recovery is put into the best perspective. When we often let the things others say and do affect us from doing positive things, we're eliminating ourselves from making the best out of our lives. Not many people close to me knew about one terrible incident in my past. I was having some difficulties in school when I was in college, so I was out of college for a while and lived in Charlotte with my God sister for that time period. I would often go to the school that she was teaching at to assist her with different things. So on one particular day she had me go pick up uniforms for her cheerleaders (she was the coach at her school at the time). On my way to the place of business I was pulled over by the police in downtown Charlotte (the license plate on her car wasn't updated so that's why I was pulled over). The officer got all of my required information like he was supposed to, then he came back to the car and informed me that there was a warrant for my arrest. Now when I heard those words I immediately freaked out, I've never been in any trouble so I wanted to know why I had a warrant for my arrest. The officer informed me that he couldn't provide any further information for me and that he had to take me to jail (the jail was literally around the corner from where I was pulled over). I felt horrible and even though they were in front of me, I

Recovery

was handcuffed and placed in the back of the police car. Only time I was in a police car was when my sister, two of our childhood friends, and I all played an April Fool's Day joke on our mothers when we were teenagers. So this three minute ride in the back of a police car was probably one of the worse experiences I had in my life. My God sister was called on her job by the police and they let her know what happened; she immediately came to the precinct. I soon found out that I had a worthless check that was submitted to my bank account for payment. I wasn't working at that time so I was confused as to how a check was submitted, because I wasn't paying for much of anything. After sitting in a holding cell for about an hour witnessing some crazy things, I was allowed to sign myself out. My other God sister's sister-in-law was a sheriff and was on duty at the time, so she checked on me periodically making sure I was doing alright. I cried the entire time I was in that place, but I was so relieved that I didn't have to be around everyone else and I didn't have to be strip searched as well. I later found out that when I was at one of my friend's houses back in Greensboro before going to Charlotte, one of my checks were stolen out of my purse and the young man that did it, did what he could to get money. So after that incident I no longer used checks and whenever I went over certain people's houses, I left my purse in the trunk of my car. I have a clean criminal record and things worked out in my favor in court following that incident. That setback didn't keep me down; I quickly recovered and continued to move on with my life. Things occur in life that we often have no control over, so instead of getting down on ourselves we need to keep pushing and live life right. I encourage anybody that goes to jail to not continue the cycle. We all make mistakes but some mistakes just shouldn't be made. We also need to learn from our mistakes as well as the mistakes that others make around us.

We shouldn't hold grudges in life; we should accept things the way they are and do what's necessary to make the best out of difficult situations. I personally don't have any grudges towards certain individuals I've come in contact with that did me wrong. I've made plenty of mistakes and treated some people wrong, so it would make me a hypocrite if I held grudges towards them and didn't expect people to hold grudges towards me for the things I've done. I recall some tough times growing up in my house in which I witnessed physical, verbal, and emotional abuse between my mother and sibling's father. I also witnessed firsthand how anger and frustration could make someone lash out with harsh language, physical threats, and then would carry out those threats on numerous occasions. My mother was a single parent who had a lot on her plate (sole provider of six children). I refuse to hold things from my past over anyone's head today because it was in the past and if I don't move on, how am I helping myself? Parents really need to encourage their children as much as possible; times get hard and frustrating but we should never treat them opposite of the way in which we want other people to treat them.

Recovery

One of my favorite movies growing up was The Jackson Movie. The Jackson family grew up in poverty and lost a lot during their childhood years, and they still had issues that followed them from their childhood into their adulthood years. They overcame major struggles and were helpful citizens to our society. That's a perfect example of recovery and how the Jackson family continued to strive for the best. Thanks to people like Dr. Martin Luther King Jr. who fought for equal civil rights for all mankind; minorities were able to recover from unequal struggles which were endured in the past. It doesn't matter where we start; the important fact in life is about where we are and where we're going. Growing up with poor self-esteem and molding myself to help those younger than me feel good about themselves, is a wonderful gift that lasts a lifetime!

This year I spoke to my four year old nephew for the first time in his life. He lives on the west coast part of the country (and of course I live on the east coast). He is half Japanese and half African American. I made the assumption that he only spoke Japanese; well I got in touch with his mother and we talked for a while (she's fluent in Japanese and speaks some English) and I was surprised that my nephew's primary language is English. My brother (Anthone) which is his father, can somewhat speak and understand other languages due to him being a Marine (often lived in other countries). I talked to my nephew on the phone for a short time due to him acting shy and not knowing me, but I enjoyed the talk and I call to check on him every now and then. If we don't take steps to make changes for the better, we won't advance or help ourselves be in good places. I have good relationships with all of my nieces and nephews and I see them from time to time, but this particular nephew I haven't gotten the chance to bond with yet. I'm thankful that I'm getting to know him and I'm making progress to take the next step in going to see him. This process of recovery is in my hands because I'm the adult and if I want to build a relationship with him, I have to start by communicating with him. Putting one foot in front of the other and taking the necessary steps, applies to all lessons in life. When or if we make bad grades in school, we have to make efforts to pull them up to satisfactory grades if we want to see improvement. When we travel and take the wrong turn, it's only right to turn around or get the right directions to get us where we need to be. When children do things to get on punishment it's only right for them to serve the punishment and not do the things that had them on punishment, anymore. Well in some cases, some children learn the hard way and test limits a lot instead of learning the first time from their mistakes. Children have to know that adults like me have been in similar situations when we were children, so we tell them to do right because we know that when we are doing the wrong things in life, they can lead us down the wrong paths. Pride gets in the way in a lot of circumstances with people; we often attempt to prove the wrong things to others. Pride causes us to dig ourselves into deeper holes in so many situations. My pride got in the way

Recovery

with me a lot from moving on to bigger and better situations in my life, but it's all a part of growing up.

I've been so independent for so long that I don't like asking anyone for help, even my family. My siblings and I never got the fancy shoes and clothes that some children got when we were younger. Six children in one household is a lot to handle and it's very difficult for one parent to provide for. When I turned sixteen and got my first job I always spent a lot of my money on clothes and shoes for my younger three siblings. They were about six, five, and three years old so nice sneakers like the fancy Michael Jordan's, weren't that expensive. I was happy to be able to buy things for them that I didn't get when I was their age. I always saw other children around me getting very nice things and at times I was jealous, but I never complained to my mother because I knew she was financially doing what she had to do to take care of all of her children. That's why when I got old enough to buy things I brought things for others that needed or sometimes wanted things that I couldn't get when I was younger; and those people were typically my younger siblings. I really don't think my pride got in the way with this topic; I was doing what I thought was right and it made me feel good. After I first started college, about a year later I got my first car. I didn't have any established credit so my father agreed to cosign for me to get my car. Well I did alright with my monthly payments for a little while then I started to slack off. I was helping my siblings and constantly traveling back and forth to

Chenelle M. Wiles

Charlotte to help them get things they needed. So as a result of this I fell behind on some car payments. Well my pride got in the way and I didn't fully explain to my father ahead of time what was going on. I didn't think he'd care because his two children he had with my mother were grown and he wasn't with my mother any longer (so he didn't have an obligation to help). My father had a good paying job, two cars, and a nice condominium. He soon made the trip to North Carolina from Maryland to get the car from me that he cosigned for. I was very upset and knew that I did wrong, but didn't understand why my father couldn't just help me. It was a learning experience and about five or six months later, he gave me my car back. I later paid that car off and that was an accomplishment for me! Some years later my father had found himself in a financial crisis and he needed my help but I didn't hold any grudge from the past against him, so I stepped up and helped him. Everyone falls down in life, so it's always good to have people (especially family) be there and put things back together. My father ended up driving the same car he took from me, when he came to live with me. Pride would often get in someone's way that was in my father's position but I didn't see it. Although it wasn't too long before the time in which he had to come live with me and drive one of my cars, that he was doing well and making good money. Nothing in life is guaranteed except death and it only takes that split second for things to fall apart. People often lose jobs, homes, and cars and go through difficulties in life without a moment's notice.

Recovery

A lot of health problems often take over our society and death often follows many of the health issues. AIDS, cancer, high blood pressure, and many other illnesses and diseases can lead to death. In my twenties I was diagnosed with high blood pressure. I always thought older people were the only ones who could get high blood pressure. Well I was wrong; many of my family members have high blood pressure and it's a health issue that runs in my family as well as many other families. A lot of people in my family know that I've never been a fan of taking medication. I've always gotten migraine headaches as an older teenager and all throughout my adult life, but I refused to take aspirin. Resting seemed to relieve my headaches (sometimes I had to rest for a few hours). When I found out I had high blood pressure and my doctor ordered me to take iron pills, I didn't like that at all but I did what my doctor recommended (well for a short period of time I did). I also inquired about my headaches and I was given tests and a cat scan of my brain but thankfully nothing was wrong, I was just experiencing stress. So the doctor ordered me to take iron pills for my high blood pressure so that it would come down. I had to take the necessary steps to get my pressure down and if I wanted to do that I needed to follow the recommendations. In the summer of 2010 I had to go to the emergency room one afternoon because I was experiencing a lot of pain in my side and stomach area. Tests were run on me and it turned out I had some issues with my uterus. I usually heard the word uterus when women are having babies but that wasn't my case, well at least I didn't think it was. I had to go back and forth to see a specialist for a few months and they performed numerous tests on me. Finally I was told that I should get the extra tissue lining that was building around my uterus removed. I was scared and didn't know what to expect at that point. I know that doctors make calls that are beneficial for patients but that call could or couldn't have been beneficial for me. I thought things out for a while and talked about it with my two older God sisters. Thank God, things began to slow down and my body wasn't experiencing much pain any longer. Even though the extra tissue lining remains, I'm thankful I didn't have cancer which I was tested for and neither did I have to have any major operations. Recovery works in different ways with different people. I can't get back the things I lost out on in my past but I can make a recovery by doing what needs to be done for myself today and for my future. When I was seventeen and busted the back of my head by riding on the hood of a car horse playing, I had to mentally recover by not making decisions to do things like that anymore. I had to physically recover by going to the emergency room and getting stitches in the back of my head. Of course I could've lost my life due to that careless decision I made, but my life was spared and better things were in store for me.

    I opened up and told my story because I know that many people go through things at various points in their lives, but many never recover. Stress has been a big issue in my life even though I'm young, but I'm still learning that I can't allow

Recovery

situations that are beyond my control, get the best of me. I also have to acknowledge that helping others can be beyond my control; my continuous help often became enabling. We can't use our downfalls as excuses to why we haven't made turn arounds for ourselves. We have to know that even though we've been in a dark tunnel, eventually light will appear. I admit there were times that I wanted to throw in the towel and send my son back into the system, but that was what he was used to. I couldn't do that to him, instead I implemented tough love, life skills, and structure into his upbringing. Many people won't admit this but in life structure is what's needed, and that applied to my son. His life today is a great example of personal recovery. It's humbling to hear him give advice to others younger than him on how to do the right thing, seeing that he put a block against a lot of help that used to come his way. I've always told him to be honest and admit to the mistakes he makes, its life. Making mistakes doesn't mean we're bad people, it just shows us that we're not perfect and we can do some things that aren't right. So if we do something different and not make those same mistakes, then we're recovering from our wrongs.

I hope when people all over the world read this book about what I've been able to do with my life, they see that it doesn't matter what we go through, we can still fulfill our destinies. I not only encourage the youth in the world but I encourage the adults to make things happen for themselves, by acknowledging where they are and where they need to go!

Chenelle M. Wiles

Adults also fall off track and make mistakes but continuing to get up and move forward is the detail role in life; adults are the key players! I admire all of the people who take care of children (no matter what your titles are), to dedicate yourselves to them on a consistent basis. Children need positive attention and want to be heard so just take time out to listen to them; they say important things all the time! When you lose important people in life to death or to the fact that they simply just walked out, judge how important they are and decide how moving on will benefit or hold you back. Just because you might not hear the words "I Love You,' doesn't mean you can't learn how to love and that love doesn't exist. When you grow up in the ghetto that doesn't mean the mentality and actions within you, have to be nothing but ghetto. We all start from somewhere so we have to take our lives one step at a time. A few words can turn into a book, a few steps can turn into a touchdown, and a couple of seats can turn into an audience full of cheers. Never judge a book by its cover, never count an individual out due to past mistakes, and never stop in your tracks because a rock is in the way. If you need help ask for it; there might be a lot of people to turn you down but there might also be one person to step in and offer to help you!

Hate is a strong word and it has a long lasting meaning to it so we should be cautious when or if we use that word. Love is also a strong word and with that same sense, we should be cautious when we use it. So this big but short thing called life

Recovery

is important and it needs to be enjoyed to the fullest. We might have physical limitations but it doesn't mean we have to limit ourselves to not reaching our fullest potentials in life. I have a six year old niece that's completely blind but she's one of the happiest little girls I've ever been around. She's full of joy and love; my older brother who is her step father explained to me that she enjoys a lot of television shows. When she sits in front of the television for one of her shows she imagines what's taking place. When people that can see often watch television, we see what's going on without thinking twice about the imaginative options that can take place. Just like my niece has a limitation, she's happy and enjoys life so we all need to have the same regard with any limitation we encounter. Life is certainly what we make it!

    I can recall numerous conversations I've had with my sister (Sheriliah) regarding the fact that she would like to know where her father is. From the time I left Charlotte and went to Greensboro for college in 1998, my sister would always talk to me about trying to find out where her father was located. She would often tell me that she was happy with her life and the success she has endured, but she also expressed the fact that she was missing out on something and that was her father. Before we moved to Charlotte in 1989, she had little contact with her father but now doesn't remember what he looks like. She knows his name but other than that, that is all she can recall. My sister often asked my mother questions about her father but she rarely ever got too many answers.

Chenelle M. Wiles

We both know that he spent some time incarcerated in Oklahoma but other than that, she wanted to know where he was. Every time my sister brought up the topic of her father, I fully listened to her because I know she wanted to find out a lot of information regarding him. There were a few times in which both of us searched the internet to see if we could locate his whereabouts, but we didn't find any leading results. During the times we traveled back to Maryland to see family, we didn't see any of her paternal family neither did we see our maternal grandmother's (Shirley) family, until years later. I continued to comfort and listen to her about her deepest concern which was her father and his whereabouts, because that was something that I knew she worried about so much. At this point in time questions are still not answered by my sister in relation with her father. I really hope one day soon she finds her father and they are reunited, just like my son was reunited with some of his biological family!

    I am on a journey in life and I will not stop succeeding in life! I know that there are situations that often come in everyone's path in life, that we often can't control. When we are in car accidents, most of the time they are out of our control especially if the accidents aren't our fault. My sister (Sheriliah) lost a good friend following a car accident. This particular car accident wasn't at the fault of her friend, it was caused by a drunk driver. That drunk driver didn't think about the fact that he was putting someone else's life in his hands due to his careless actions. Her daughter was left

Recovery

without her mother; situations like that do not have a recovery ending. Another death that was caused by someone else was dealing with someone that I considered as family; she was distant cousins to my younger two siblings. She lived just two doors down from us in the same neighborhood we lived in for seven years(Boulevard Homes). I can recall times in which she, my sister (Sheriliah), and I would often play together as children. In 2007 bad news devastated the Charlotte NC area, everyone in our community, and more importantly her family, when her life was taken away by a man. He didn't think about his actions beforehand and the fact that her young daughter would be without her mother, as well as the rest of her family. This is another example of how a situation didn't have a recovery ending.

    My higher power is God and He has a plan for everyone, we just have to be willing and able to walk the plan that He has made for us! I know that many people believe in different higher powers but I'm thankful for my true belief in God! I have attended numerous churches all throughout my life but one understanding I do have is that Jesus sacrificed his life so that we could all have eternal life. I might not be that person in church who does all of the yelling, I might not even be one of the people who runs around the church shouting, but I do have a relationship with God! I also know that He is the Highest among all High so I will thank Him in advance, during, and after all of my many blessings! I'm far from perfect , I've made mistakes, and will continue to make mistakes.

I want to be willing and able to share my story with not only the people in my family, teachers/professors, friends, people I grew up with, mentors, mentees, and coworkers, but I want people all over the world to be able to put their positive ambitions into action by letting them shine! It generally takes one time for information to be passed on to millions of people and stored in safe keeping for a long time to come. For the information stored in this manuscript that I created: I hope it will be stored in so many people all across the world! The little vision I had some years ago to write a book, turned into reality! This is only the beginning of my journey with writing books, I will soon be on my next mission by writing my second book! I am not just writing about information that occurred in my life, I'm encouraging the many people in this society that think there is no way they can make their dreams come true; I'm letting you know that DREAMS DO COME TRUE!!!!! None of us can change the past but we can make changes for our present and for our future! Hopefully the changes you make in your life will be positive changes! Even when the going gets tough, find some joy and Faith and let that define your inner most desires! Always try to eliminate talking down on others and to yourself; replace those words with uplifting and loving words! Words may not hurt some people but when someone that is important to me talks down to me or curses me, it hurts because we're not supposed to harm the people we love and care for!

Recovery

This is not a "Tell All" or a document I produced in which people should feel sorry for me due to any situation I described in this book. It simply opens up anyone's eyes, mind, heart, and soul to not judge anyone or take anything for granted. This material is a part of the journey in my life; whatever positive endeavors follow, I'm willing to make it another footprint in the milestone.... **Chenelle M. Wiles**

LIFE

Life

In my opinion life is many things. In a weird way life's unpredictability can be predicted very easily from experience, as a child my mom unknowingly taught me a lot about universal law and how the energy you put out into the world will find its way back to you. It's funny how one day you can feel as though everything is as bad as it will ever be and the next day it gets worse. At the same time when you have beliefs (whatever they may be) you give yourself a sense of security which usually manifest itself when you least expect it. Life is also circumstantial in how we all come from different situations and backgrounds but in many cases have the same aspirations. Life can be a lesson in itself in how it can take someone the majority of their lifetime to realize what is really important to them. Life can be misleading or obvious, life can be troubling or joyous, life can change permanently in an instance or stay the same forever.

Omari Hunt (Former Basketball Player/Mentee)

32 Years In

Life can best be illustrated as an autobiography customized with treasured memoirs. As the narrator of my own book, I summarize life as a collection of valuable personal experiences (excerpts) expressed daily on a new page. It's always easier to write the beginning, as a child life seems so perfect and gentle. As you drift closer to the middle, your understanding becomes tainted and blurry. After a while, the chapters get longer, as the readings get more tiresome. For me it's been 32 short years and I have been blessed with nothing but success. Even more, I have an extraordinary family support system that has lifted and guided me throughout my way. But, I too have experienced that point in your life where you have reached your plateau and things start to move in slow motion. Similar to nearing the end of a book and suddenly you get drowsy and can't finish. But what motivates us to complete the readings? What motivates us to live? What inspires us to do well and make those essential decisions that we make for ourselves and our families? Those are the questions that will sum up your autobiography making sense of the carefully written pages and allowing others to discover the true meaning of life and what it's worth through your interpretation.

Nikki Ballentine (friend)

Life

Life is not always pleasant but it is what it is. It does not always give you what you want but most times it gives you what you need. It will always be a learning lesson for all. You have to take life day by day and try to make it the best you can.

Katrine Wiles (mother)

Gift of Life

It is said that there's no greater gift than the gift of life. Thirty-two years ago I was given my first of two gifts in a form of a wonderful son. The second gift came eighteen months later, which was a beautiful baby girl. Life has its good and bad moments, but life in itself is a gift and I'm very grateful for it.

Theodore "Teddy" Wiles (father)

Life

Life has not been the easiest but growing up and going through the things I went through, helps me look at things a different way. Life is meant to be exactly what the title says: LIFE!

Demontay Wiles (son)

Life to Me is about Paying it Forward

In order to better understand WHO I am today, I must reflect upon WHERE I come from.

Success in my life as an adult has everything to do with how I was raised as a child, and fortunately for me, I have wonderful childhood memories. My family includes 1 younger sister, 1 half-sister, and 2 loving parents that were both teachers, so every day was a "teachable moment" in our household. They were supportive & right there at every football game I cheered in, & dance recitals I performed in for 13 years.

I grew up watching my mother spend countless hours at the kitchen table working on lesson plans for her 3rd graders as she would strive for perfection, and I admired her passion and dedication to the teaching profession. My father was a high school teacher at the school I attended, and was greatly admired as he lead many clubs and organizations and often served as a mentor to countless young lives in our community. Both my sister and I were destined to take the same path as our parents have passed the torch.

My very first job at the age of 14 was an assistant dance instructor at Nina's School of Dance in Durham, NC, where I attended for many years, and it was during that time that I learned a great level of discipline and commitment for something I loved to do. By the age of 16, I was hired as an afterschool dance instructor, and that's when I officially knew that my calling was to work with children and I shared the same passion that was deep in my family roots. In 1987, I attended North Carolina A&T State University where I received my bachelors' degree in Early Childhood Education, and I'm proud to say that I have enjoyed over 20 years in the teaching profession.

I was hired in Charlotte Mecklenburg Schools at the age of 22 as a 6th grade teacher in April of 1992. Needless to say the school year was almost over, but I was overjoyed to get a job! The principal created a class for me by taking 5 students from each 6th grade classroom, and I was told that these students were "good kids" that would perform better in a smaller classroom setting. My classroom was the conference room right next to the principal's office & she wished me good luck.

I was eager and ready to make a difference, and had only 2 full months to do it. I can remember building my first relationships and sharing many laughs, and great stories about their lives. I held many contests to challenge students to do their best as we prepared for final testing and even purchased small prizes as rewards for them. I quickly learned the power of incentives and was amazed at how hard they were willing to work for someone that truly believed in them. I was extremely grateful for completing my first assignment, and gave big hugs and smiles and wished that group of students well as they were moving on to a new school that next year, and thinking that I would never see any of them again.

It wasn't until a few years later that I was in contact with Chenelle, a former student, from that first small group. She was able to locate the school that I had transferred to & she told me that she always thought of me and wanted to know how I was doing. I was so excited to see that she was doing well in high school because I remembered that she was one of the students in that small group that appeared to be different in her own unique ways. She was very quiet and shy, but an excellent student that I believed would have a bright future. We spent a lot of time catching up and I gave her my home phone number so that we could stay in contact. Over time, she became like a younger sister, my *"God sister"* and I wanted to show her the world. Our "upbringing" was very different, and I knew that her circumstances did not allow her some of the same opportunities that I had, but I wanted her to see life through my eyes. I took her to get her hair and nails done and we would go shopping and share many laughs together. Before I knew it, years had passed by, and I knew all of her siblings and mother very well. I got married; Chenelle graduated from high school, and my daughter was born. By that time, she was a part of my family and I had introduced her to my parents and younger sister. I always knew how important family was to Chenelle and learned so much from someone that was 11 years younger than me. I admired how she worked at an early age and made many sacrifices to help take care of her younger siblings, and I knew that she would be a great aunt to my daughter, & became affectionately known as Aunt CoCo. One of my proudest moments was when Chenelle realized she wanted to be the first in her family to go to college, and was enrolled in my alma mater….Aggie Pride!

I have found the many rewards of teaching & coaching to be the absolute best part of my job, and knowing the influence that I have on students and the power to impact or change lives motivates me to be a better person every day.

Becoming a teacher has been one the greatest gifts that God has given me, and I feel that it is my duty to "pay it forward" and pass on my blessings to others by helping to mold and shape the lives of so many wonderful and talented students just like "my Coco". **LaShawn Summers (God Sister for life)**

LIFE

What Is Life?

Life to me is everything!
Life is not always easy so that makes it a challenge!
Life is a battle so you have to fight for what you want!
Life is filled with frustration and pain but nothing a human can't deal with!
Life is a puzzle so take that chance and solve it!
Life is everything and everything is you!
God put us on this earth for a reason so dance the dance of life and just live it!

Natasha Little (God sister of Chenelle and younger sister of LaShawn Summers)

LIFE

Life Is Living Learning Loving and Laughing

Life has many facets; you only have one chance at life. It's no rehearsal; therefore one must live life to the fullest. Truly work hard because in the end life is what we make it. You have to pray, live it, learn it, and laugh through it. You also learn to love; one who can't do it isn't living it to the fullest. Life is often tough; most people struggle to get by to educate themselves, getting homes, and so much more. Hard work is rewarding in the end, which enables us to have the better things we want. Put God first, have trust, faith, and go for opportunities that avail to you. Focus on your strengths and let go of the negative so you can deal with positive people and situations. Life is not a bowl of cherries; it's not fair but it is what it is. God may not come when we want Him, but He's always right on time. It takes strong parents to raise children, even for single parents. Keep a good sense of humor; laughing is healthy. Music, poetry, and peace and quiet deep down in your heart is what's needed in this thing called life. Take care of yourself; being healthy is important and without good health there is no life.

David and Carolyn Turner (parents of LaShawn Summers and Natasha Little)

Life

Life is a bunch of hills. As soon as you get over one hill then comes another. As a kid some might say that life is a playground or a sandbox, but life is no easy climb!

Mya Greene (12 year old daughter of God sister LaShawn Summers)

Life for Me

Life for me is just the beginning. I just graduated from college, hoping to land my dream career by trying one day at a time. I have a plan for my life, but everyone knows plans change. My life is full of love, and surrounded by loved ones. Life has thrown me curve balls, and I had to deal with them on my own but always with the guidance of those who care about me. My life is very exciting and I look forward to the future. You have to keep the faith, because it can get hard out here with the change in the economy and the mean people in the world. In life I have dealt with pain, heartache, happiness, sadness, but the most important thing out of all is that I'm blessed to be living. One day I hope to share my life with someone, and create a life of my own.

Patrice C. Robinson (mentee since age twelve)

LIFE

The Father in Me

I had to learn to be a father by stepping up the same way people have to do with "On the Job Training." I had the best intentions, yet I made mistakes. My plan was to be the best I could be and give my children a basis from which to parent and build on my parental success. I also had to improve my mistakes and set the right example for my children. When this life is over all we will leave is our legacy of how we treat ourselves and others. Life is a journey so enjoy the straight a ways and the curves!!!

John Reynolds (father of mentee Tiaera Reynolds)

Life

Every day I wake up and there's this thing called life the fact that I'm breathing seeing and eating every day it's just a piece of the big pie Sometimes you go through obstacles that make you grow to come out alright It's not about the finest thing or materialistic object but about the well-being and knowledge to wake up every day and say I'm alive This morning I woke up with bills on my mind hard to say but that's an everyday thing that I can't seem to shake Yea I brush my teeth and wash my face but it's a brand new day a day that I seek survival The nicest memory couldn't compare to the fact that I'm living You may look across the street and wonder that car I would dare to drive That outlet store I dare to shop in The

LIFE

jewelry that person has around their neck is one of life's commodities Why wonder when you can grab it Not financially but mentally it's a rhinestone and you can have it To find in this here stack of hay a diamond in the rough is a treasure you finally reached when you successfully found yourself People go on day to day trying to put on some type of facade or imaginary life that they cover up with the nice clothes and fly rides Why spend all of your money on things that will one day be gone like the tides on a shore A sore loser never comes back for more A champion comes back to even the score A successful person knows that a scoreboard can't award the world's largest trophy That's only to be shelved and never looked at anymore Life is precious to create life is a blessing Life is taken advantage of sometimes We don't realize how good we have it until one day it's all taken away and given to a new owner to charade I have my flaws we all do but instead of pointing them out embrace them learn and throw the bad habits away Family is a big part of life Yea people say they came in this world alone so that's how they're going out that's kind of a fiction statement because if you were so alone and can do everything on your own don't ever need a shoulder to lean on you never would've been brought to life Life is so you can learn from the people around you grow from the things you're not supposed to get into and be stronger than yesterday for all the things and people that hurt belittled and taken advantage of you Choose your meaning and open your eyes Everybody has a purpose on this earth and it starts with you breathing for the first time It is what you make it either use and build yourself into another successful individual or mold and rot and never mentally be able to say I'm alive I can say I'm alive whether good or bad my smile is bright as the sunshine that's why I have life. B.Wiles

Nise Wiles (sister)

Twenty-Seven and Living

What does life mean to me? Wow out of my twenty-seven years of life no one has ever asked that! Life to me is living every day as my last, making sure to be thankful for everything that God has blessed me with; my children Elijiah and Samara, my family, and my friends. Life to me means making a difference in my children's lives as well as others. Life also means leaving a great legacy for my family to want to pass on. Life is just treating people how you want to be treated. Life is giving everything I do, my all!

Sheriliah Robinson (sister)

11 & Already a Star

In May 2011 I was awarded the MVP of the Right Moves for Youth for my school's basketball team. I love playing basketball and this year was my first year at my elementary school and in the Right Moves for Youth Program. Right Moves for Youth is not only about being a basketball player on a team but... "I will do my best to tell the truth obey the rules respect myself and others be drug free and help others make the right moves for a better life for all." I loved being the leading scorer and playing my position as a center. That's why I'm 11 and Already a Star.

Elijiah Lockhart (nephew and son of Sheriliah Robinson)

Dreaming Big

I dream big about doing my best in school every day. I dream big about dancing and moving to one beat. I dream big about one day becoming a cheerleader and a rock star. I dream big about graduating from elementary, middle, high school, and college. I dream big about being a good person in life and getting into the Right Moves for Youth Program when I get to the fifth grade, like my big brother did.

Samara Lockhart (7 year old niece and daughter of Sheriliah Robinson)

LIFE

Philosophy of Life

I met Chenelle in October of 1993 at Jackson Park Baptist Church. She was thirteen years old, shy, and a little standoffish. She knew I saw something special in her and that I'd eventually make her hug me (she wasn't affectionate. She lived in Boulevard Homes in Charlotte NC where my son (Officer John Burnette, Charlotte Mecklenburg Police Officer and the Community Coordinator). She knew John and his other two partners (Officers Andy Nobles and Mike Adams). Community Policing started in Charlotte in August of 1993 & John was one of the first Community Coordinators. Their Team patrolled 9 neighborhoods on the Westside of Charlotte, introducing themselves to the residents & developing relationships. The Children were very important to them & Boulevard Homes was a major area of concern due to the drug activity there. On October 5, 1993, My Families World changed forever. Our son Officer John Burnette & his partner Officer Andy Nobles (Charlotte Mecklenburg Police) were murdered in Boulevard Homes by Alden Jerome Harden, a crack cocaine user & who had been on robbery sprees over the past week to get money to buy his drugs. When John & Andy arrived at the scene, Harden ran & the Officers were in pursuit. John got to him first & they got into a tussle. Harden was able to get my son's gun out of John's holster & he shot both of them in the head. Harden was found guilty on two counts of first degree murder & was sentenced to Death Row on August 12, 1994 & Harden is still there today. When bad things happen to you, God brings other people in your life. **I thank God for bringing Chenelle to me** & 17 ½ years later we are still best friends & will be until we go home to be with Our Lord. We have been through many things together & are both stronger because of them. **I am so proud of all of her accomplishments & especially for her loving a dear young Man, Demontay, who is now her Son & my Grandson.** I am honored that she asked me to write about "My Philosophy of Life." As a Child, much like Chenelle, I grew up in a dysfunctional family. My Dad had a great job as an Engineer with Seaboard Railroad & was also a musician, which also lead him to be an Alcoholic. He was very handsome & my Mom was very insecure & jealous. Being the Middle Child, I became the **"Peace Maker"**. Regardless of the situation, I always saw the positive side & tried to make things better for everyone involved. I was introduced to the Lord as a young teenager by my Best Friend's Mom. I accepted the Lord when I was 13 years old. Some people still say I am the **"Peace Maker"** at age 60.**I trust my Lord & I know he does not make bad things happen**. Everything is **ALWAYS** on His Time. He created everything & everyone. We are all his Children! He Loves us unconditionally & if he can love me this way, I feel I am to love others unconditionally, honoring him. I strive to **"Be Open"** to them, be a **"REAL Person"** to everyone God places in my path & to help them in any way I can. I believe **"In a Hand Up, Not a**

Hand Out "My Philosophy is to **"Sow Love"**, **"Reap Love"**, **"Pass It On"** & **"Continue the Circle over & over all the days of your life"**. We are to **"Be a strand in the chord of Love that Binds"**, holding it together by Love Passed Down. **"Each One Reach One!!"** "Show Love and watch it "Grow, Mend, Repair, Heal & Manifest." Life provides us the opportunity to be generous to all – and we are commanded: **"To Always Give More Than We Take!"** We must also Forgive; Forgive Ourselves & Forgive Others as He has Forgiven Us. Accept people where they are now & Love them for who they are, unconditionally. My Prayer is when I go Home to be with My Lord, **He will say "Good Work My Precious Child, My Awesome Servant & Welcome Home"** I also Pray that the ones left behind will say **"Her work on earth is done"**. **"She always left every situation better than she found it"**. **"Thank You for Giving to the Lord!!!"** So My Friends, **"Love God, Love Yourself & Love All People; Unconditionally. Live Life to the Fullest, Have Fun & share yourself with whoever enters your world!** Put everyone before yourself, asking God to Use you for his Glory. **"Every Life You Touch Will Touch You Back"** Chenelle & I have shared a fulfilling, loving life together because God " **knew I needed Her Special Touch!"** & what a precious touch it is!! "That's How He Works". I would give anything to have my Sweet John back but **I would never want to give My Chenelle back!!** She is My Gift from God, My Child & she also provided me with another Grandchild, Demontay!

LIFE

Trisha Norket (mother of the late Officer John Burnette and special friend)

The Meaning of Life

The meaning of life to me: As we walk through this portal called "Life" we learn that there are so many lessons to be learned as we teach others from the "Tests" and "Trials" that we have been given so this may help or encourage someone during their time of "Testing." Life is full of rewards despite the struggles accompanied by tears, long days, and nights. Life is a gift that keeps on giving. Once you experience love, love takes on a life of its own that never dies, even after the loved ones are gone.
 I love you Chenelle M. Wiles. I am so glad that God has given us the opportunity to share the same "loving" yet a "little crazy" family. Our history extends from the coast of West Africa to the coast of the Pee Dee River outside of Anson County in North Carolina. This will be one of many books to come in the nearby future.

Stephanie H. Teasley (cousin)

Life

I don't know where to start. Life is crazy one day you look up and it seems as if half the people you know have gotten married, had children n bought a house with a two car garage in a picket fence. I've learned that even though I don't have much I have everything I need. I've learned to stop basing where I am now on how far the next person has gotten. I don't believe there is anything wrong with positive motivation but I don't condone feeling down on myself because other people have surpassed me. I look at it like "you don't know what they had to do to get where they've gotten"(they could cry every night-be in a horrible relationship-be behind on all their bills etc.). So when you think the grass is greener on the other side of the street, don't go buy a new house, just water your own.

Billy Ferrante (friend)

P.S. Life is very short so live it to the fullest and treat others the way you like to be treated...

Much Love,

Chenelle M. Wiles

June 2011

Following the completion of this manuscript, we lost the lovely Sandra Swann (Greensboro NC): Thank you for your unconditional love, support, and dedication to your family, friends, and coworkers. We Love and Miss You... R.I.P (6/26/67 - 8/23/11)

www.ingramcontent.com/pod-product-compliance
Lightning Source LLC
Chambersburg PA
CBHW050642160426
43194CB00010B/1772